NM4 FF

Achieving Successful Returns from Care
What makes reunification work?

Achieving Successful Returns from Care
What makes reunification work?

Elaine Farmer, Wendy Sturgess,
Teresa O'Neill and
Dinithi Wijedasa

BAAF
ADOPTION
& FOSTERING

Published by British Association
for Adoption & Fostering
(BAAF)
Saffron House
3rd Floor, 6–10 Kirby Street
London EC1N 8TS
www.baaf.org.uk

Charity registration 275689 (England and Wales)
and SC039337 (Scotland)

British Library Cataloguing in Publication Data
A catalogue record for this book is available
from the British Library

ISBN 978 1 907585 25 8

Editorial project management by Shaila Shah, BAAF Publications
Designed by Helen Joubert Designs
Typeset by Avon DataSet Ltd, Bidford on Avon
Printed in Great Britain by TJ International
Trade distribution by Turnaround Publisher Services,
Unit 3, Olympia Trading Estate, Coburg Road,
London N22 6TZ

BAAF is the leading UK-wide membership
organisation for all those concerned with
adoption, fostering and child care issues.

Contents

List of tables

List of figures

Acknowledgements

The Department for Children, Schools and Families (now the Department for Education) funded this study as part of the group of research projects funded under the Quality Protects initiative. We are very grateful for this assistance and would particularly like to thank our research liaison officers, Dr Caroline Thomas and Dr Carolyn Davies for their invaluable assistance and for thinking that it was important to find out more about reunification.

We are extremely grateful to the six local authorities that allowed us access and introduced us to children and their parents. In particular, their administrative staff made our lives considerably easier by being well organised and extremely efficient. Team managers and social workers made us welcome, facilitated the work and were interested in what we were doing. We are also indebted to the children, young people and their parents who talked to us at length and shared their experiences with us.

Regular meetings with our Research Advisory Group were valuable and we would like to thank Helen Jones and Jenny Gray from the Department for Education, Ian Sinclair, Harriet Ward, John Simmonds from the British Association for Adoption and Fostering, Robert Tapsfield now with Fostering Network and then with Family Rights Group and John Gumbleton, private specialist reunification practitioner, for giving their valuable time to help us with this work.

We would also like to thank Julie Selwyn and Dinithi Wijedasa for their generous help with the analysis of the children's outcomes, Paula Morris who worked so hard on the data collection, and Carol Marks who provided an extremely efficient, fast and accurate transcription of the interview tapes.

During the writing of the report one of the authors, Dr Teresa O'Neill, died after a long illness. We are indebted to her for her contribution to the whole study, for her in-depth practice knowledge and also for her personal contribution to the research team. She is very much missed.

We have tried to represent accurately the different experiences and views of reunification in this book and also convey some of the complexity of the issues. However, if there are any errors they are solely our responsibility.

Notes about the authors

Elaine Farmer is Professor of Child and Family Studies in the School for Policy Studies at the University of Bristol, prior to which she spent several years as a social worker in England and Australia. She has researched and published widely in the areas of child welfare and child protection. Her recently completed studies on reunification, kinship care, adoption and neglect were part of research initiatives funded by the Department for Education. Her books include *Trials and Tribulations: Returning children from local authority care to their families* (1991), *Child Protection Practice: Private risks and public remedies* (1995), *Sexually Abused and Abusing Children in Substitute Care* (1998), *Fostering Adolescents* (2004), *Kinship Care: Fostering effective family and friends placements* (2008) and *Adoption Agency Linking and Matching: A survey of adoption agency practice in England and Wales* (BAAF, 2010).

Wendy Sturgess was a Research Associate in the School for Policy Studies at the University of Bristol. She worked on a large adoption study prior to looking at reunification. Before joining the School she worked on the ALSPAC (Children of the Nineties) study. Her background is in psychology.

Teresa O'Neill was the Director of the Post-Qualifying Award in Specialist Social Work with Children and Young People and had a particular interest in children's rights, youth justice and gendered practice within these systems. She had extensive child care practice experience and had worked as a team manager and children's guardian. Her PhD thesis was published as *Children in Secure Accommodation: A gendered exploration of locked institutional care for children in trouble* (2001).

Dinithi Wijedasa is a Research Associate at the Hadley Centre for Adoption and Foster Care Studies at the University of Bristol. In 2005 she carried out a national level research project to standardise a developmental screening test for Sri Lankan children. Since joining the

Hadley Centre in 2007, Dinithi has been involved in a range of research studies, including pathways to permanence for ethnic minority children; educational support services provided by independent foster care providers; an evaluation of a new model for providing adoption services; adoption and the inter-agency fee; and transition to adulthood for adopted young people. She is a co-author of the book *Pathways to Permanence for Black, Asian and Minority Ethnic Children* (BAAF, 2010) and co-authored a chapter in *The Child Placement Handbook* (BAAF, 2009).

1 Background and research issues

Introduction

Whilst there has been an increasing amount of research information about admitting children to care and about their placements once there, information about returning them to their parents has remained scarce in the UK. This is a curious situation since the most common outcome for children who enter care is return home. This neglect of research attention to reunification is mirrored by a lack of clear guidelines and ideas for practice. As a result, reunification[1] has been in some ways an invisible – yet high risk – area of work.

Before the Children Act 1989, there were three studies of a sub-population of returned children, that is, those placed with parents under a care order or "home on trial" as it was then known (Thoburn, 1980; Farmer and Parker, 1991; and in Northern Ireland Pinkerton, 1994) and one study of all kinds of return (Bullock *et al*, 1993; revised and reprinted, 1998), that also used pre-Children Act data. In addition, Trent (1989) conducted an action research project which pointed the way to effective reunification practice. Research conducted in the 1980s showed a rate of readmission to care from parents of about a quarter (Rowe *et al*, 1989; Bullock *et al*, 1993).

Although the Children Act 1989 heralded a new emphasis on family support and on the reunification of children with their birth parents, there has been limited research evidence about reunion in the UK since its introduction. One study suggested, however, that the rates of children returning to care after reunification were twice as high as was the case prior to the Children Act 1989 (Packman and Hall, 1998). As a result, concerns have been raised about the impact on children of "oscillating" or moving repeatedly between home and care (Bullock *et al*, 1993; Packman

---

1 In this book, the term "reunification" will be used to denote return to one or both birth parent/s from care and the words "return" and "reunion" will also be used interchangeably.

and Hall, 1998) and about the persistence of optimistic expectations about return (Ward and Skuse, 2001; Farmer and Lutman, 2009; Ward, 2009).

In addition, unsuccessful returns are driving some of the instability of looked after children (Sinclair et al, 2005). In order to achieve greater stability for children, there is a need for a deeper understanding of how to increase the level of successful returns, which supports are crucial to success, over what period and in what circumstances return is contra-indicated. The study reported on in this book set out to fill some of these gaps in our knowledge.

Research on reunification

Until recently, much of the up-to-date information on reunification in the UK came from studies on substitute care. In addition, a useful project on return has been conducted by the Who Cares? Trust (2006). More recently, Wade and his colleagues (2011) have compared maltreated children who go home with those who do not. There is a much more substantial body of research on reunification in the US, although these findings should be used with caution because of the rather different context and child welfare systems in the US (for reviews of this research see Biehal, 2006 and Farmer, 2009). In this chapter we sketch in the background to the study on which this book is based and provide a brief review of the relevant research.

What leads to children returning to their families?

Some children enter care only briefly, for example, when their mothers go into hospital and they return quickly and without major problems. However, for other children return will depend on parent–child relationships improving, on changes in a child's behaviour or on social workers believing that the safety of previously abused or neglected children is now assured. Perhaps it is not surprising then that voluntarily accommodated children have been found to be three times as likely to be returned to their families as those placed under care orders (Cleaver, 2000).

UK research (Dickens et al, 2007; Sinclair et al, 2007; Wade et al, 2011) has shown that there are also local authority differences, with some local authorities being more willing to return children to their parents and deal with a higher level of risk in so doing than others (possibly related to having more support services to offer), and that in those authorities which took such risks there were more failed returns. In addition, it has been found that there are differences between teams within authorities as to the chances of children returning home (Sinclair *et al*, 2007; Wade *et al*, 2011).

Research suggests some factors which relate to the likelihood of children being reunified:

Parental problems

US studies have shown that a variety of parental problems are associated with a lower probability of reunion, including poverty, housing problems, parental drug misuse and chronic mental illness (see e.g. Goerge, 1990; Rzepnicki *et al*, 1997). Reduction of the parental problems that led to care and an assessment that the risks to children are at acceptable levels have also been found to be important predictors of return home (Wade *et al*, 2011).

Contact

Earlier studies suggested that the maintenance of contact between children and their families was the 'key to discharge' from care, that is, to return home (Aldgate, 1977; Fanshel and Shinn, 1978; Millham *et al*, 1986). However, further investigation of these findings has shown that contact significantly predicted return home only during the first six months of placement in the Millham *et al* study. Indeed, when Quinton and his colleagues (1997) re-examined Fanshel and Shinn's research, frequency of parental contact only accounted for a very small proportion (2–5%) of the variance in return rates at their four follow-up stages.

Cleaver's study of contact (2000) suggested that contact alone was often insufficient to promote a child's return home. Direct work on existing attachments and work on the problems which led to care were often also needed. Nonetheless, infrequent contact with birth parents is linked to a lower likelihood of maltreated children returning to their parents (Wade *et al*, 2011).

Motivation

Parental motivation to care and willingness to change contribute to return and its success (Bullock et al, 1998; Cleaver, 2000; Harwin et al, 2001; Sinclair et al, 2005). Some parents are motivated to take their children back by the view that their children are behaving better or have matured but other returns occur because parents or children decide on reunion and make it happen – often because of parental concern about the lack of boundaries around children's behaviour (especially in children's homes), because children have been harmed or abused in care or because the parent and child cannot manage the separation. Earlier UK studies (Thoburn, 1980; Farmer and Parker, 1991) highlighted that parent or child determination often provoked reunification, especially in the absence of clear plans by social workers. Parent or child insistence on reunion then sometimes does, and at other times does not, signal positive motivation to make return work.

Little has been written about children's attitudes to return. However, when Skuse and Ward (2003) interviewed reunified children, they found a concerning picture of returns characterised by a lack of formal support. In addition, the young people consulted in the The Who Cares? Trust project (2006) often felt that their views had not influenced the decision for return and would sometimes have preferred a more "incremental" approach to reunion, involving increasing contact with their parent/s, more consultation with themselves and contingency planning that would allow them to return to care if the return did not work out.

Nonetheless, in Wade and his colleagues' study (2011), maltreated children were cumulatively less likely to be returned home if the records showed that the child had accepted the need for care or did not want to return home, as well as if the parental problems that had led to care had not resolved or if the child had a learning disability or had been neglected.

Caregivers

Caregivers play a largely unsung role in the return process. Placement caregivers may contribute to reunification if a foster placement breaks down or residential staff demand a child's removal (Vernon and Fruin, 1986). In other situations, caregivers, rather than precipitating returns, may work closely with parents to encourage return and mentor parents who may feel more able to trust them than social workers who hold the power to remove their children (Farmer and Parker, 1991; Child Welfare Information Gateway, 2006). Unfortunately, caregivers sometimes find that planning for return happens outside the review process, so that they do not have sufficient opportunity to help children prepare for returning home and some see themselves as an untapped resource (The Who Cares? Trust, 2006).

Return to parents from kinship care

Research from the UK and US suggests that reunification with birth parents happens less frequently from placements with family or friends than from unrelated carers (see e.g. Rowe et al, 1989; Wulczyn and Goerge, 1992; Scannapieco and Jackson, 1996). This is probably partly because placements with kin have often been used where the prospects of return are remote (see e.g. Farmer and Moyers, 2008).

The timing of return

Studies in the UK, US and Australia have consistently found that the probability of reunification is greatest immediately following placement in care and that the likelihood of return to parents declines as time in care increases (see e.g. Fernandez and Delfabbro, 2010; McSherry et al, 2010; Wade et al, 2011). For example, Sinclair and his colleagues (2007) found that 61 per cent of children who returned home did so within six months. Of course, the length of time children spend in care before return is due to a variety of factors so these findings do not mean that remaining in care for longer than six months in and of itself reduces the chances of return, as Biehal (2006) emphasises in her review of research on reunification (see also Stein, 2009).

Research has also suggested that shorter stays in care may be associated with rapid return breakdown (see e.g. Wulczyn, 1991; Davis et al, 1993), possibly because insufficient change took place before return was attempted. Wade and his colleagues (2011) too found that the returns home of maltreated children were more likely to be continuing at six months when the children had gone home slowly over longer periods of time.

Pressures for return

Much research assumes that reunification is in the gift of local authorities, but often it is not. UK studies have shown that in reality planned reunifications unaffected by pressure from the child, the parents or the substitute care placement, are very much the exception rather than the rule (Thoburn, 1980; Farmer, 1996).

Planning and purposeful work towards return

A UK study of children in foster care found that the return of children to their families was frequently poorly planned and supported and often occurred as a result of a series of placement breakdowns (Sinclair et al, 2005). Researchers in the US have also found that reunion is often un-planned (McMurtry and Lie, 1992). Moreover, US research suggests that all too frequently reunification occurs without resolution of the problems that led to initial placement in care (Turner, 1984; Barth and Berry, 1987; Fraser et al, 1996) and consequently children re-enter care.

Biehal (2006) reported on two experimental studies of specialist reunification projects in the US which showed that focused case planning is an important means of achieving reunification. The Alameda study concluded that social workers need to take an active role in planning for children's futures as soon as they enter care. This project used written contracts to agree clear goals with parents (Stein and Gambrill, 1977, 1979). The Family Reunion Service study also found that the involvement of parents in joint planning and the setting of objectives were vital ingredients of the project (Walton et al, 1993).

In the UK, Trent's action research project (1989), which used permanence with adoptive families as the model for reunification work, had promising results and again showed the importance of providing focused work within specified timescales combined with clarity about the consequences if goals were not achieved. Other researchers have provided valuable research-based models of reunification practice (Maluccio et al, 1986; Thoburn, 1994).

Harwin et al (2001) in the UK found that planning the return of children is particularly difficult in cases where mothers misused drugs or alcohol, as in other respects these parents were often viewed positively. In a subsequent study, Forrester and Harwin (2004, 2008) point to the need for improved access to treatment resources and much more training for social workers in the recognition of substance misuse and in making realistic assessments about prognosis that will not be overwhelmed by "misplaced optimism".

Indeed, Maluccio and Ainsworth (2003) suggest that family reunification practice needs to be reshaped to address the issue of parental drug misuse. These authors describe a number of relevant US projects, including initiatives where alcohol and drugs specialists are co-located with children's services, and note that without the imposition of requirements to become involved in treatment, many parents are unlikely to do so. They also highlight the need for time limits for reunification when the time needed for parental recovery does not keep pace with children's developmental needs and with the requirement to protect them. In the UK the Family Drug and Alcohol Court Project provides a useful model of active court work with substance misusing parents in care proceedings (Harwin, 2009).

Outcomes of reunification

Re-abuse

In an earlier study (Farmer and Parker, 1991), we found that a quarter of all the "protected" children (that is, those who were younger and at risk) were neglected or abused after returning home. This re-abuse rate was in line with those found in other studies of children in high-risk situations at that time (Barth and Berry, 1987; Farmer and Owen, 1995; Gibbons et al, 1995; Brandon et al, 2005).

A more recent three-year follow-up of 596 children in foster care in England found (as might be expected) that children who were returned home were significantly more likely to be abused than those who were not returned (Sinclair et al, 2005). There was strong evidence of re-abuse for 11 per cent of those reunified with their families and some evidence in a further 31 per cent of cases.

Given these figures, there is a need to investigate whether this apparent rise in re-abuse rates has been maintained and what can be done to improve children's safety.

Psychosocial outcomes

There is considerable evidence to suggest that children reunited with their families often experience worse psychosocial outcomes than those who remain in long-term care or are adopted (see e.g. Taussig *et al*, 2001; Sinclair *et al*, 2005; Biehal, 2006; Farmer and Lutman, 2009; Davidson-Arad, 2010). Wade and his colleagues (2011), for example, have shown that the outcomes for maltreated children who remained looked after were better than for those who were returned home, with respect to both stability and children's wellbeing. In particular, they found that children who had been neglected did best if they remained looked after.

These studies raise difficult questions about what standards are acceptable when children are returned home, how far services can offset some of the disadvantages of poor parental care, and whether children's services are intervening soon enough when standards fall unacceptably low (Sinclair *et al*, 2005). Biehal (2006), in her review of the research evidence, commented that more research was needed into the risks and outcomes associated with reunification. These are issues which this book addresses.

Return breakdown

One UK study, which focused on children admitted to care under voluntary arrangements, found a breakdown rate of half (52%) of all returns, with 24 per cent of the children experiencing more than one reunion (Packman and Hall, 1998).

Other UK evidence comes from a study of a sample of new entrants to care, of whom 15 per cent of the 133 children discharged home returned to care within two years (Dickens *et al*, 2007) and from a study of a cross-sectional sample of children in foster care, of whom 37 per cent of the 162 children who returned home re-entered care within three years (Sinclair *et al*, 2005). Wade and his colleagues (2011) found yet higher levels of return breakdown, with only a third of the maltreated returned children in their study remaining continuously at home four years later. Farmer and Lutman (2009), in their five-year study of neglected children returned to their parents, found that 65 per cent of their returns had disrupted. There is therefore a pressing need for more information about what leads to return breakdown, what can be done to prevent it and about children who experience repeated return breakdowns.

Factors associated with return breakdown

There is plenty of evidence that return breakdown is associated with older age at return (see for example Rowe *et al*, 1989), longer periods in care (Fein *et al*, 1983; Farmer, 1992) and with poor prior planning (Block and Libowitz, 1983). These factors are similar to those associated with foster care and adoption breakdown (Fratter *et al*, 1991; Berridge, 1997; Sinclair, 2005).

It appears too that the extent of movement experienced by children during separation can compromise the chances of the return lasting, especially changes of placement (Block and Libowitz, 1983; Packman and Hall, 1998). Changes in the composition of the child's birth family in the child's absence – especially changes in the other children – have also been found to have a disruptive effect (Farmer, 1996; Packman and Hall, 1998). It is therefore important that children retain a sense of belonging and their possessions at home remain untouched while they are away. Bullock and his colleagues (1993) emphasised that the return of children to their families is a process that is as stressful as that of separation and intimately connected to it (see also Maluccio *et al*, 1994).

In the US, African-American children have been found to be more likely than white children to experience disrupted returns (and to have spent longer in care beforehand) (National Black Child Development Institute, 1993). In the UK, Barn (1993) considered that the differential treatment of black and minority ethnic children and their parent/s affected return patterns.

Packman and Hall (1998) found that return breakdown was more likely when the initial separation was due to parental mental illness or alcohol or drug misuse, no doubt because these problems often recur during reunification (see also Schuerman *et al*, 1994). Limited parental skill too is associated with disrupted returns (Hess *et al*, 1992; Davis *et al*, 1993; Courtney, 1995) as is neglect as the presenting problem (Hess *et al*, 1992; Davis *et al*, 1993; Courtney, 1995). In Packman and Hall's (1998) study of accommodated children, difficulties during reunification were related to children with a tendency to violence or self-harm. Problems with schooling, including truancy and school exclusion, also affect the success of reunion (see also Lahti, 1982; Farmer and Parker, 1991).

Much research on return considers all children together, yet the issues for younger at-risk children (the "protected" group in our 1991 study) and "disaffected" teenagers are often rather different. Nonetheless, previous failed returns home have been found to be related to return breakdown for both groups of children (Farmer and Parker, 1991; Wulczyn et al, 2000).

In addition, there is some evidence that return breakdown is associated with lack of support from the extended family, friends and neighbours (Festinger, 1994). However, it is important to note that high levels of formal support and services are not in themselves sufficient to maintain reunions. Much depends on the content and mix of services provided (Block and Libowitz, 1983). Similarly, research in the UK has highlighted the important contribution that proactive social work, decisive planning and continuous social work involvement can make to successful reunification (Trent, 1989; Farmer, 1996).

A US study, based on a review of 62 case files of children whose returns disrupted, highlighted problems arising from lack of social work time to work with families as well as poor social work assessment (Hess et al, 1992). In this study, Hess and her colleagues found that social work plans were poorly implemented or children were returned where parents did not comply with substance abuse treatment and that, even where they did comply with requirements, this did not always result in behavioural change. There was widespread over-optimism about the degree of parental change and an assumption that reunification was best for children.

Indeed, one UK study of children in foster placements found that repeated efforts were sometimes made to return children home, even when this was not in their best interests (Sinclair et al, 2005; see also Farmer and Lutman, 2009; Wade et al, 2011). Once they returned, the children rarely received further social work intervention or support (Sinclair et al, 2005). Similarly, Ward and her colleagues (2008) found that only a quarter of the children in their study had contact with a social worker after their return home. For others, contact with a social worker often centred on practical issues and rapidly tailed off. Wade and his colleagues (2011), however, found that when maltreated children were returned to their parents they received more services in the first six months than children who remained in care.

At a practical level, The Who Cares? Trust project (2006) noted the importance of holding a review before children go home when return occurs as a result of a change in the care plan and recommended that a multi-disciplinary panel is needed to approve return decisions and determine the support needed, with accountability at a senior level.

Gaps in knowledge

Overall, then, the research evidence suggests that reunification carries high risks and that the chances of return breakdown are high. Most of the research in the UK was carried out a long time ago or return was not the main focus. Much useful research has been conducted in the US but it is not clear how far those findings apply in the UK. There is therefore a real need for up-to-date information to enable local authorities to make informed decisions about when to return children to their parents and what kinds of services and case management will increase the chances of success. The study reported in this book examines these issues and also explores children's progress for two years after return in order to identify the key factors that predict whether reunification is likely to be successful, in what circumstances children are likely to be re-abused, and what leads to some children oscillating in and out of care. In addition, the study explores how the social workers, parents and children involved experience return and what they say would help them.

2   Study design and methods

Aims

This study aimed to find out more about the reunification of looked after children with their parents and had three broad aims:

- to examine the patterns and outcomes of return home through a two-year follow-up of a large sample of returned looked after children;
- to investigate which factors are associated with successful and unsuccessful returns;
- to explore through in-depth interviews with children and parents their own experiences of successful and unsuccessful returns, including repeated failed reunification ("oscillation"), the understandings they form about these and the impact of these experiences on them.

Design

The study was based on a consecutive sample of 180 children, aged 0 to 14, who were all returned home from care in six local authorities in England during a one-year index period. The researchers examined the progress of these reunions over the following two years. The two-year follow-up period was chosen as long enough to demonstrate a good range of outcomes of return.

The first (or only) return during that period was selected as the "study return" and was defined as:

> *Return home to a parent or parent figure (step-parent/parent's partner or adoptive parent) when the child was either discharged from care or placed with parents under a supervision order, interim or care order.*

The period of care preceding the study return is referred to as the index care period.

The following children were excluded from the sample:

- Children aged 15 or over at the time of the return;
- Children who had only been looked after for six weeks or less, *unless* they re-entered care within one year;
- Children who were looked after only as an agreed respite arrangement.

Children aged 15 or over were excluded from the sample so that, at the end of the two-year follow-up period, the sample children were 16 or under and thus both their educational outcomes (whether or not they were still attending school) and the outcome of the return (whether or not they came back into care) could be properly considered and also because the issues for care leavers going home are rather different from those of other reunified children. Children who had only been looked after for six weeks or less were excluded as those returns were likely to have been relatively unproblematic and, if they were not, then the children were included in the sample if they re-entered care within the one-year index period. The returns of children in respite care were also excluded, as these were likely to have been of a different nature to other reunions because of the short period of separation and the frequency of return. Aside from these exclusions, in each participating local authority all of the children who returned home during the one-year index period were included in the case file study sample until a total sample size of 180 children had been reached.

The sample of 180 children was drawn from six local authorities; one London borough, one metropolitan district, one unitary authority and three county shire authorities. Authorities were located in London, the Midlands, the southeast and the southwest and two had a substantial proportion of black and minority ethnic children.

The Management Information Team within each local authority was given detailed instructions on how to select children eligible for inclusion in the study. Study invitation letters, consisting of an introductory letter from the local authority, an invitation to participate in the study from the research team and two information sheets, one for children and one for parents, were then sent to parents. The Norah Fry Research Centre and the Reading Recovery Centre in Bristol advised on the "readability" and design of these. Where parents and children were living together, the study invitation letters were sent to parents; where they lived apart, letters were sent to both parents and young people (if they lived independently) or to children's carers. Once access to the case files was agreed, the children's names and social worker details were forwarded to the researchers.

Case file review

Information was collected from the case files of the 180 children who came from 141 families. This included demographic information, their background histories, the adversities and maltreatment experienced by the children, their behaviour and development, the services provided for children and their parents, contact with parents during care, and how the cases were managed. Data were recorded about three distinct periods in the children's lives. These were the period from the child's first referral to children's services until they entered care (for the index care period before the study return); this care episode itself and the study return, including the children's progress over the two-year follow-up period. This information was recorded on a schedule designed for the study on which we recorded 330 items of information, with an accompanying coding manual specifying clear rating criteria for the relevant variables. In addition, a lengthy summary covering the whole progress of the case was completed on each child.

Information on the returns was examined in depth so that the outcome of reunification could be considered both in terms of its stability (whether at the end of the two-year follow-up period it was continuing or not) and its quality – defined as follows:

Good quality – Returns that were positive or adequate for the child. This category included cases where there were some difficulties or adverse incidents but, on the whole, circumstances for the child were adequate or good.

Borderline – Returns that included circumstances or incidents that were likely to be harmful for the child *or* where the parent was having difficulties managing the child, but we did not consider that the return should have ended, either because the difficulties were not sufficiently serious or because, on balance, care would not have been a better option for the child.

Poor quality – Returns that were unacceptably harmful for the child and/or significantly limited his/her life chances, such that either they had ended, or in our opinion should have been ended, *or* where the parent was totally unable to cope with or contain the child's behaviour.

These three outcome groups will be referred to as the "good quality", "borderline" and "poor quality" groups.

It should be noted that case file information has certain limitations. Some of these relate to data that are not routinely recorded on files (for example, the reasons for some decisions and receipt of benefits) and others to information that is found on some but not other files, so that there may be missing data on particular issues. In addition, case file records are by definition the social workers' constructions of events. Nonetheless, we found them to be a rich source of information about the children, parents and placements and they allow access to the whole range of the population under study, which is not possible with interviews. This study aimed to capitalise on the strengths of these two sources of information.

Interviews

In the second stage of the research, semi-structured interviews were undertaken with a sub-sample of children and their parents. As far as possible, both the children and their parent/s were interviewed about their experiences, although this was not possible where the children were too young to interview (aged 8 or less) or where either the parents or children did not wish to participate. Brief telephone interviews were also conducted with the children's social workers or team managers. Interviews were conducted with parents, children and social workers relating to 37 (21%) of the cases from the case file sample, as can be seen in Table 2.1. In just under half of these cases the returns had been successful, whilst for the remainder they had not.

Interviews were conducted with 34 parents (of whom three talked about the returns of pairs of siblings). Twenty-seven interviews were held with mothers, three with fathers and four with both parents or a mother and her partner. About half the interviews covered children who had been under 10 and the other half those aged 10 or more at the time of the study return.

Table 2.1
Interviews

	Child, parent and social worker	Parent and social worker	Child and social worker	Parent and child	Parent only	Child only	Total no. of cases & interviews
Number of cases	11	10	1	5	8	2	37
Number of interviews	33	20	2	10	8	2	75

Nineteen interviews were conducted with young people, 16 of whose parents we had also interviewed. At the time of the interviews, the children were aged between eight and 18, including two who were under 10. Six were boys and 13 were girls. Separate help and advice lines information sheets were given to all parents and children at the conclusion of the interviews.

The 22 telephone interviews with social workers and team managers covered 23 children. At the time of the return just under half of these children had been under 10 and just over half above this age. A further six social workers had been contacted and agreed to take part but were then unavailable at the times arranged for the interviews, and five others declined to participate.

Eighteen of the social work interviewees were women and four men, with the majority in the 40–49 age group (11). Six were under 40 years old and five were over the age of 50. All except one leaving care worker held a social work qualification and nearly three-quarters (16) had more than 10 years' post-qualification experience, with three having two to five years' experience and the remaining two less than two years. The majority were located in children and families long-term teams. Only some of the interviewees had been directly involved with the child and parent(s) at the time of the study return, while others had worked with the child on a subsequent return or at a later stage or were managers with only indirect knowledge of the families.

The interviewees, particularly the children, sometimes chose not to (or were unable to) answer particular questions, so when the interview findings are reported the number of responses will not always add to the full number of interviewees. All the interviews were recorded and transcribed with the permission of the respondents and all identifiable information encrypted on computer to maintain confidentiality. The parents and young people who took part in the interviews were given a store voucher as a small token of thanks for the time they gave to the study.

Interview schedules

Semi-structured interviews combining a "qualitative" approach to questioning with a "quantitative" treatment of data were developed to yield both systematic numerically analysable data and extensive case material. The broad structure used for the case file review was followed for the parent, child and social worker interviews but adapted as appropriate for each.

Parent interviews

Parents were asked about contact and services whilst the child was in care, about the decision for return and preparation for it, how reunification had worked out in practice, the support and interventions provided and how the return had progressed. If the return had ended, they were asked about its ending and what might have made things work out better.

Child interviews

When their parents agreed to participate, children aged eight and over were asked if they were willing to be interviewed. If they gave consent, the interviews with them followed closely the structure of the parent interview but also incorporated two more age-appropriate approaches to information gathering. These were a Life Trail or Storyboard at the beginning of the interview to ascertain the child's perception of the moves they had made and an eco-map towards the end to depict their view of their closeness to family members and others.

- *Life trail or Storyboard* – Children and young people were presented with two alternative ways of depicting their life story. The *Storyboard* was an A3 page divided into a number of large consecutive boxes, with

17

each box representing a different place the child had lived. For each place the child was asked how old they had been when they lived there, with whom they had lived there and why they had moved from there to the next place. Older children tended to use this method to write out their life events giving explanations for each move without much need for prompting from the researcher.

Most younger and several older children preferred to use the *Life trail* to depict their story. This measure was developed with the help of a graphic designer and used a large colour illustration of a broad wood-land trail as the canvas for the child's story. Colour stickers depicting different animal homes (for example, a fox's den, spider's web, bird's nest) were then stuck onto the life trail to represent the different places the child had lived. The child then wrote onto each sticker how old they had been when they lived there and with whom they had lived there and explained to the researcher why they had moved from there to the next place.

Once the children had completed the *Storyboard* or *Life trail*, the researcher asked them to identify up to three words that best described how they had felt whilst living at each place, using "feelings" cards (happy, sad, thankful, guilty, angry, lonely, etc). These responses were then coded later in the interview.

The *Storyboard* or *Life trail* remained prominent for the rest of the interview so that the researcher could visually point out the index care period or study return to the child when asking about these (i.e. 'at the time when you were living here with so and so' or 'when you went home here').

- *Eco-map* – a simplified version of the Four Field Map (Sturgess *et al*, 2001). This was a drawing of concentric circles with the child at the centre. Children were asked to write in the names of the people in their lives and to place them in one of the circles, depending on how close or distant they felt from them.

During the course of developing the children's interviews a group of young people were consulted about the materials and format and their views informed the final form of the interviews.

Social worker interview
The telephone interviews with social workers focused on similar issues to those in the parent interviews but also included the planning and support provided for the return and social work judgements about the impact of services, the reasons for return success or breakdown and the impact of oscillation on children. Finally, social workers were asked for their comments about social work practice in returning children home from care.

Analyses

The case file material was analysed using SPSS for Windows. In the analyses small variations in sample size across tables are not commented on unless the reasons for the missing data are germane to the analysis. When correlations were examined to look for statistically significant associations, Chi-square or Fisher's Exact Test (two-tailed) were used and relationships were considered to be significant where $p<0.05$, which indicates a relationship beyond the 5 per cent level of probability. Analysis of variance (ANOVA) techniques were used with interval variables to compare average values (means) between the two groups (e.g. length of time in the placement). Further details about the analysis of outcomes are given in Chapter 10. It should be noted that exact levels of probability will be used sparingly in the text but any relationship described as significant or to which we draw attention should be assumed to be statistically significant unless stated otherwise.

In what follows, the names and some of the details of the individuals who are described have been changed in order to preserve confidentiality.

Policy discussions

Interviews with senior managers were conducted in the six participating local authorities to discuss current policy and practice relating to reunification. At that time, none of the local authorities had formal, written policies on reunification, although there were some general statements about a commitment to the principles of the Children Act 1989 that children should be looked after within their own families wherever possible.

Priority and resources for reunification

There were differences between the authorities in the priority and resources allocated to this aspect of social work practice. For example, one local authority had recently piloted a scheme aimed at reunifying more children, particularly adolescents, through the provision of a package of family support services. Several managers in different authorities said that they thought social workers would benefit from some specific training to prepare them more effectively for the task of promoting and supporting children's return home, and to try to change prevailing attitudes, which they felt were resistant to children going home.

Placement with parents on care orders

At the time of the study returns an average of 12 per cent of all looked after children in England were placed with parents under The Placement with Parents Regulations 1991. Three of the authorities in the study for whom figures were available had a somewhat higher than average proportion of children placed with parents (14%, 18% and 21%), whilst in contrast another of the authorities had none. The latter authority had had the experience of the death of a child on a care order following reunification with parents, since when it had rarely returned children on care orders.

One authority attributed its large number of children at home on care orders to a "safety first culture" where care orders were made instead of supervision orders, even where there was no intention of removing the child from home. Sometimes the courts, with the support of children's guardians, made care orders rather than supervision orders to ensure the provision of family support services. Indeed, one authority, in which the number of children on care orders living with their parents was nearly twice the England average (and which was described in an SSI inspection report as "risk averse"), attributed this to very cautious children's guardians who recommended care orders even when social workers had recommended supervision orders, and who were reluctant to support the discharge of care orders.

A third authority had found that, in a quarter of cases, where children lived at home on care orders, a recommendation for discharge of the care order had been agreed, but no progress had been made towards this, partly because of the time this would have taken. In addition, there was the issue of children who "drifted" home following a series of placement break-downs, where the local authority was unable to exercise the order but would be unlikely to be successful in seeking to discharge it.

Care planning

General concern was expressed in all authorities about whether and to what extent social workers were using care plans proactively to work toward children returning home in a planned way. It was suggested that, particularly with older children, unplanned reunification was frequently initiated by the children or their parents, sometimes when a child remained at home after contact or an overnight stay and refused to go back to their placement. In such circumstances social workers were left with little alternative but to "condone" the return even if services to support reunification were not in place.

Budgetary pressures for return

Managers in several authorities suggested that, where departments were experiencing financial pressures, children could be returned home as a means of reducing the cost of out-of-home placements, especially expensive specialist (often out-of-area) placements. Similarly, children placed in out-of-area independent fostering agency placements were sometimes brought back to less costly placements within the authority which, if they subsequently broke down, resulted in the child's return home. In contrast, resource problems, such as a shortage of reviewing officers, could result in few children returning home within short time-scales.

The timing of returns

Identifying the "right time" to work toward reunification appeared to present authorities with some difficulties. In one authority there were particular concerns about children who were settled in foster placements and appeared to be doing well, but as a result were "stuck" in the system with little motivation on the part of social workers and foster carers to work towards them returning home because of the disruption it would cause (and the loss of income for foster carers). In another local authority concerns were expressed both that children remained in care too long before a return home was attempted and that children stayed too long in their families after return, when there were severe difficulties, before returning to care.

A manager in one authority suggested that reunification should always be attempted, except in cases where it was clearly contra-indicated, because even it if was unsuccessful it could be constructive in that it would give the child the opportunity to test out what may be an idealised view of their parents and home situation against the reality.

Family Group Conferences

Family Group Conferences were identified by managers in three local authorities as an important facilitator in the reunification of looked after children. In practice, we found little evidence of the use of Family Group Conferences for the children in this study, so we are unable to report on how well they work in this context.

Support

Family support workers played a major role in providing support to families following children's return home, and some authorities were attempting to give this area of work greater priority. For example, one authority was in the process of refocusing support services away from looked after children and towards supporting children at home and returning home, and another was implementing family support plans with supervision orders to keep children at home as an alternative to care orders. However, managers in three authorities expressed concern that when services and budgets were under pressure, support services provided to families following children's return home could be affected and provided at only a minimal level, if at all.

Oscillation

An issue of concern which was raised in several authorities related to children who had returned home after being looked after (sometimes with care orders still in force), only for new problems to develop resulting in repeated breakdowns and requests for a return to care on the basis that they were beyond parental control. These children, who were often older, experienced increasing instability as they moved back and forth between home and care placements, and presented difficulties for local authorities trying to keep them out of the care system, for parents who could not manage their behaviour and looked to the local authority to take responsibility, and for the children themselves.

These issues highlighted by the managers identified a number of policy and practice areas that were shown by the study to be shortfalls or practice dilemmas, as we shall see in the following chapters.

Now that the study's methodology and the local authority context have been described, in the next chapter we examine the early experiences of the children.

3 The children's early experiences

This chapter describes the children's experiences from the time they were first known to children's services up to their entry to care (for the index care period which immediately preceded the study return). It includes the characteristics of the children and their parents, the parenting the children received, the parents' circumstances, information about child protection referrals and previous periods in care.

The parents' histories

The childhoods of the children's parents had often been troubled and just over half (52%) of the mothers had been abused or neglected when they were growing up, whilst just over a quarter (28%) had been in care themselves. Information about the birth fathers was sparse, but at least 14 per cent had also experienced maltreatment and at least a tenth had spent time in care.

Children's services departments had been involved with almost half (49%) of the families before the child in our study became the focus of attention, including a fifth (21%) where children had already been taken into care or been adopted. Half of the mothers had had their first child when they were still teenagers.

In a high proportion of families, children were exposed to domestic violence (67%), substance misuse (59%) or adverse parental sexual activity (such as prostitution, open use of pornography or having multiple partners) (15%), with most children (82%) exposed to one of more of these. Domestic violence and substance misuse were especially likely to occur together (36%) and parents could be so pre-occupied with their own needs that they were unable to meet the needs of their children.

Over half (52%) of the mothers to whom the children were returned had mental health problems. Information about the mental health of the fathers or father figures to whom the children were returned, whilst scarce, had been noted in 11 per cent of cases. Similarly, recording about parental learning difficulties and physical health problems was also variable, but at least 10 per cent of the mothers and 5 per cent of the fathers to whom children returned had severe learning difficulties and similar proportions of mothers and fathers had a physical health problem or a disability.

The children's characteristics

The 180 children in the study came from 141 families. There were 26 sibling groups, one of five children, two of four, six of three children and the rest were sibling pairs. Fifty-nine per cent of the children were boys. The children ranged in age from 0–14 at the time of the study return and 16 per cent were from a minority ethnic group. A small proportion (14%) had a physical disability and nearly a quarter of those aged four or over had had a statement of special educational needs, as can be seen in Table 3.1.

Table 3.1
Characteristics of the children in the case file sample

No. of children	180 from 141 families
Gender	106 boys (59%) 74 girls (41%)
Age (at return)	Range 0–14. Mean 7.72 years (5.01 s.d.)
Ethnicity	152 white (84%) 28 (16%) had black and minority ethnicity backgrounds of whom 21 were of mixed ethnicity
Nationality	177 British (98%) 3 other (2%)*
Disability	26 children had a physical disability (14%)
Special needs	31 children had a statement of special educational needs (23% of children aged 4+ at the start of the index return)
Siblings	65 children had siblings in the sample (36%)

* Of which 2 were asylum seeking.

The children rarely entered care from two-parent families (17%). More left behind a single parent, usually a lone mother (55%) or one parent and a partner (26%) and a small number (3%) had been living with a parent and another relative, usually a grandparent.

Adversities and maltreatment before children entered care

Professional concerns about the children typically began early. Almost half (48%) of the children had been referred to children's services by the age of one, including a quarter (26%) referred before or immediately after their birth, due to concerns about their parents' difficulties or parenting capacity. Four were immediately placed in mother and baby foster placements with their teenage mothers and several more moved to mother and baby residential units.

By the time they started school, almost three-quarters (72%) of the children had been referred to children's services (see Figure 3.1), usually as a result of domestic violence, concerns about the child's development or behaviour, or suspected child maltreatment.

Figure 3.1
Age children first referred to children's services

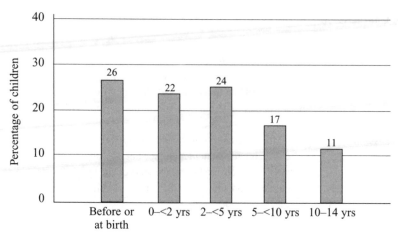

Families had been known to children's services for on average three years 10 months before the index care period (53% had been known for three years or more), but in contrast a fifth (22%) had not been known to children's services until six months or less before the children were taken into care (see Figure 3.2).

Figure 3.2
Time known to children's services before the index care period

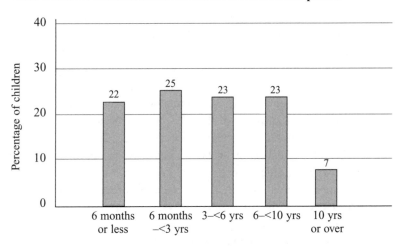

By the time they entered care, there were concerns that 91 per cent of the children were being abused or neglected. Neglect had figured for 68 per cent of the children, mainly in relation to concerns about inadequate supervision, young children left home alone or found playing out on the street unsupervised, children arriving unkempt or hungry at nurseries or schools, and children's basic needs for warmth or safety not being adequately met. This neglect was rated by the researchers as severe in 16 per cent of cases where the children were abandoned by parents, lived in extremely unhygienic or unsafe environments, or had injuries that had not received the urgent medical treatment they required.

Physical abuse of the child or a sibling had been reported in 61 per cent of cases. Severe physical abuse resulting in burns, broken bones or head injuries was a feature of 11 per cent of cases. Emotional abuse (which included witnessing domestic violence) was also an issue of concern for 61 per cent of the children. This included persistent verbal cruelty, hostility or criticism of the child as well as repeated rejection or victimisation. Some children (12%) were singled out for rejection and treated differently from their siblings (see Quinton *et al*, 1998). Serious emotional abuse or neglect (including, for example, failing to meet the child's emotional needs by completely ignoring them) was reported in 23 per cent of cases.

For over a quarter of the children (28%) there were reports of sexual abuse of either this child or a sibling. (In 18 per cent of the sexual abuse cases the suspected perpetrator was someone who had been convicted of offences against children.) Three-quarters of the children (76%) suffered or were considered to be at risk of more than one form of maltreatment, usually neglect combined with one or more other types of abuse.

For each child a measure of the total number of adversities experienced prior to the index care period was constructed. This was a count of the number of difficult parental behaviours they had been exposed to (domestic violence, drug misuse, alcohol misuse, adverse parental sexual activity and poor parenting skills), the number of forms of abuse they had suffered or been at risk of (neglect, physical abuse, emotional abuse, sexual abuse or exposure to a person who had been convicted of offences against children) and the number who had experienced a parent's death (10 children (6%)). Only five children (3%) had not experienced any of these adversities, whilst three-fifths (59%) had experienced between five and 10 (see Figure 3.3). The average number of adversities experienced by the children was 4.8 (s.d. 2.1).

Figure 3.3
Number of adversities experienced

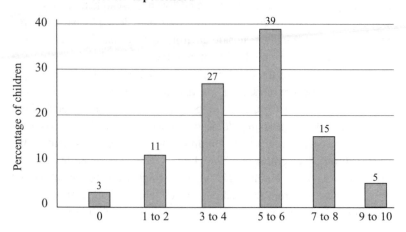

Just over half (52%) of the children had been subject to a child protection plan at some point before entering care on this occasion, with a third still subject to a plan. Referrals about child protection issues (other than those that had led to these plans) had been made about almost two-thirds of the children (64%), with 17 per cent of the children having been made subject to an interim care order, care order or supervision order at some point prior to the index care period.

Two-fifths of the children had been in care previously, once (23%), twice (11%) or three or more times (5%) or had been in a series of respite care placements (14%) before entering care on this occasion. One child had already been in care nine times. Indeed, as we will see in Chapter 11, more than a third (38%) of the children had already experienced one or more previous returns home from care.

Moreover, many children (30%) had lived with friends, a member of their extended family or their other parent at least once prior to the index care period and a few (5%) had moved more frequently between these carers. For 37 per cent of the children this meant that they had experienced two or more changes of household prior to the index care period. Only 46 per cent of the children had not experienced any such moves, so there had been considerable instability for a good number of the children before they entered care on this occasion.

The parents' perspectives on their situation before the children entered care

The interviews with the 34 parents helped to illuminate their experiences before their children entered care. As we will see, they had encountered a range of problems.

A past history of difficulties

In three of the 34 parent interviews, the children were looked after because of the parents' prior difficulties. For example, in one, the mother only discovered at the time her baby was born that the father had seriously assaulted another child. This mother went into a mother and baby unit and broke off her relationship with the father. Another mother who had physically abused her first child had alerted children's services when she fell pregnant again and was admitted to a mother and baby foster placement for assessment.

Alcohol and drugs misuse

Eight of the 34 parents explained that they or their partners had problems with alcohol misuse, with one also mentioning drug use. Only three were admitting to their own alcohol problems, whilst the other five were describing a partner who drank or took drugs or both. We know from the case files that at least another nine of the parents whom we interviewed had drink and/or drug problems. There was little reference to treatment or help with drinking problems in the interviews, with the exception of one mother who had in-patient treatment, another who saw a specialist substance misuse worker and a third who had talked to social workers and staff at a clinic. Parents' lack of openness about their own difficulties with alcohol and drugs and the lack of treatment were important issues which emerged as the study progressed.

Domestic violence

Of course, substance misuse difficulties were often combined with other problems such as difficulties with the children's behaviour, neglect and domestic violence. Nine of the parents described domestic violence (in five of which there had also been alcohol or drugs misuse) and this had sometimes been the issue that precipitated the children's entry to care. For example, Mrs Smith's baby had remained with her on the express understanding that if there was more domestic violence the baby would return to care. When the police were later called out to a violent incident, the baby was removed from her and her partner.

Mental health problems

Nine mothers reported that they had had mental health problems before their children became looked after. Eight of the nine had suffered from depression, including two mothers who had been treated in in-patient units for considerable periods. Two had suffered from post-natal depression and had not been able to attend adequately to their babies, who did not put on weight and became withdrawn. One mother had been hearing voices and had threatened to take her own and her child's life. A few of these mothers commented that either they had not told their social worker about being depressed or that they had done so, but it had not been taken on board.

Health problems

Four of the mothers described having serious health conditions, not all of which had been noted in the case files. One mother had a health condition which had left her in a wheelchair and unable to manage three demanding children, one of whom was suspected of having ADHD. She also became depressed and saw admission to care as being the solution to these difficulties in order to give her a break. Another mother was epileptic and had severe endometriosis; a third was in chronic pain and on morphine for injuries she had suffered previously from her violent husband.

Learning difficulties

Three of the 34 mothers had learning difficulties. One of them went to a mother and baby foster placement to learn how to look after her baby and the return (that is, when they went into the community) was successful. The second lived with the child's violent father who drank heavily and the baby was admitted to care because of his violence. In the third case, the child entered care because the mother was drinking and leaving the children unsupervised. Neither of these latter two returns were to be successful.

Physical abuse

Six of the 37 children had been looked after because of physical abuse. Three were removed after physical abuse by the father and three after abuse by the mother. Two of the injuries caused by fathers were part-icularly serious, including a case where a small baby suffered fractures.

Sexual abuse

In the parent interview sample, there was only one case where an incident of sexual abuse was closely connected to admission to care (see also Farmer and Pollock, 1998). In this case, Nona had been sexually abused by a relative. This had a major impact on Nona and her family. Even though therapeutic work on the abuse was provided for Nona and her parents, she began to self-harm, ran away, took drugs and was excluded from school. Her parents were no longer able to cope and she was admitted to a children's home.

However, the interviews revealed that another seven children had suffered sexual abuse and the files had reported sexual abuse to an additional three of the children. In some of these cases, behaviours that became a major problem may have been partly connected to the earlier sexual abuse (see Smith, 1995; Farmer and Pollock, 1998). For example, Robbie entered care at the age of 11 because he was beyond control, had assaulted another child and set fires. He later disclosed that he had been sexually assaulted by a gang of boys and had also been sexually abused by a relative when younger. It was noticeable how rarely these histories of sexual abuse appeared to have been taken into account in attempts to understand the children's later behaviour or provide intervention to assist them.

The children's behaviour

In 17 cases parents said that the children's behaviour had been the main problem that had precipitated entry to care. A number of mothers described children who had always been difficult to manage and their enduring feeling that something was wrong with the children. As one mother said:

I just wanted somebody to find out what was wrong with her.

Jason's mother told us that he had had learning and behavioural difficulties from a young age. At the age of seven he had assaulted his mother and had been diagnosed with oppositional defiance disorder and ADHD and prescribed Ritalin. Julia, even when small, had rages at her mother, would wet herself and become hysterical. She also had panic attacks and later self-harmed. Her mother had mental health problems and found parenting a child very hard.

Adolescents were often described as aggressive and verbally abusive and some turned their violence on their mothers and siblings or smashed up their homes or schools. Grant had tried to stab his mother, would throw things and offend. He was on medication for depression and at the age of 14 had a mental age of eight.

Some young people were particularly hard for their parents to understand. Tina, for example, overdosed several times and her mother felt at her wits' end:

I knew there was a problem and I kept begging people to help me.

Other children clearly had a very difficult relationship with one or both parents and their difficult behaviour appeared in the context of high levels of parent–child conflict and rejection.

A number of parents expressed their relief when these children entered care. One mother said that she had dreaded it whenever her daughter came home. Six mothers said that the children had been looked after in order to give them a break. In one of these cases, what started as respite care to give the mother a break became a three-year stay in care, because the child's behaviour had proved so difficult.

Of course, as we will see, the children themselves entered care with a variety of feelings. Whilst the parents thought that a few had welcomed the break from difficult family relationships, many thought that their children had been apprehensive and some that they had felt blamed, rejected and unloved.

In the next chapter we move on to consider how children got on when they became looked after.

Summary of the children's early experiences

- The children's parents had often had difficult childhood experiences and a fifth had previously had children taken into care or adopted.
- Domestic violence, substance misuse or adverse parental sexual activity featured in 82 per cent of the families and mental health problems affected over half of the mothers.
- Concerns about the children typically began early in life with a quarter referred to children's services by or at birth and almost three-quarters referred by the time they started school. Concerns about abuse or neglect (91%) were very frequent.

- Just over half of the children had been made the subject of a child protection plan at some point *before* the index care period and earlier care proceedings had resulted in care or supervision orders in 17 per cent of cases. Many of the children (54%) had previously been in care or been looked after by relatives.

The parents' perspectives on their situation before the children entered care

- The parents described how their own problems or their children's difficult behaviour had led to care.
- The behaviour of many of the children was described by their parents as having been difficult from an early age and parents often struggled to understand 'what was wrong with them'. In many cases, there were very difficult relationships between the children and their parent/s and some parents felt relief when the children left the family to be looked after.
- Children were reported to have felt apprehensive, with some feeling to blame, unloved or rejected.

4 The children whilst they were looked after

In this chapter we consider the children's experiences while they were in care before returning home. We describe the reasons why the children became looked after, their legal status at that time, their experiences of different placements and the contact they had with their families.

The children's ages

By the time the children entered care on this occasion, a third were under 5, a quarter (26%) 5 to 10 and the largest group (41%) were aged 10 or over. A small number (7%) had entered care within two weeks of their birth, mostly straight from hospital.

Occasionally children had been removed from home by children's services or the police but more often parents struggling to cope because of their own relationship difficulties, poor mental health, addiction or illness had asked relatives or children's services to look after the children. Often at that time there had been a noticeable increase in concern about the children and their families. Children had disclosed abuse, professionals or neighbours had highlighted child protection concerns, social workers had noted a worsening of circumstances, or parents with hard-to-manage youngsters had become more insistent in their demands for a break.

Why children entered care

We examined the main reason for the children entering care. Concerns about abuse or neglect figured prominently in two-fifths (39%) of the cases; parental problems, inability to care or a parent–child relationship breakdown were the principal issue in almost half (45%), and the child's difficult behaviour was the main reason for entering care for 15 per cent. The key issues affecting parents' ability to care were their physical or mental health, drug or alcohol problems and a breakdown in the relationship with a child or partner, often including conflict or domestic violence. Often care was needed for more than one reason and when secondary reasons are also taken into account, abuse or neglect figured in more than half (53%) of the cases as a reason for children going into care and parental problems in 81 per cent (see Table 4.1).

Table 4.1
Primary and secondary reasons children became looked after

	Primary reason (n = 180)	Secondary reason (n = 180)	Total (n = 180)
Abuse or neglect	39%	21%	(53%)
Parental problems, stress or illness	45%	51%	(81%)
Child's behaviour	15%	15%	(28%)
Other	1%	2%	(4%)

NB. Figures in brackets are not column totals as cases have only been counted once where, for example, different forms of parental stress or illness were the primary and secondary reason for the child becoming looked after.

Secondary reasons add up to 89 per cent as in 11 per cent of cases there was no secondary reason.

Children looked after with siblings

Of the 180 children, 138 (77%) had been living with siblings before they went into care. Of these, almost half (46%) were looked after alone. Most of the remainder were placed with some or all of their siblings. Some children who had siblings who remained at home found this extremely painful and wished to be treated the same as them.

Legal status of the children at entry to care

The majority of the children had been voluntarily accommodated (59%), although two-fifths had been taken into police protection (14%) or removed under an emergency protection order (7%), care order (5%) or interim care order (13%). The remaining two per cent had been remanded to local authority accommodation or sentenced to time in a secure unit by the juvenile courts.

Children had been taken into police protection when they had been left at home alone or abandoned in public (usually by drunk, substance misusing or arguing parents) or where officers had been called to a volatile home situation and considered it necessary to remove the children for their safety. Children's services took out emergency protection orders (EPOs) in similar circumstances or where there were grave child protection concerns, such as non-accidental injuries without adequate explanation or the presence of a person in the home who had convictions for offences against children.

The children who had been removed under care orders or interim care orders tended to be older (average age 5.6 years) than those experiencing emergency removal (average age 4.5 years) but significantly younger than those who had been voluntarily accommodated (average age 8.7 years) or remanded to local authority care by the courts (average age 13.3 years).

The children's placements whilst in care

Placement stability was generally high, with half of the children remaining in the same placement for the whole of the care period and a third (32%) moving only once. However, the remaining 18 per cent of children had moved between two and six times. Sometimes moves were planned to provide a more stable or suitable placement, but unplanned moves, because of unforeseen carer circumstances or the child's challenging behaviour or absconding, also occurred.

By the end of the period in care, most of the children (71%) were in foster care, but eight per cent were living with relatives or friends, another eight per cent were placed in children's homes, with a few in residential schools, therapeutic treatment centres or secure accommodation. Eight per cent were living with one or both of their parents in either residential family assessment centres or a mother and baby foster placement (where the return was regarded as being the return of the family to independent living).

Children placed in residential settings (residential homes, residential schools, treatment centres or secure units) were older at entry to care than children in kinship or foster care and stayed longer in care (average 18 months), as can be seen in Table 4.2. The average length of time in care for all the children was 10.3 months, with a range from under one month[1] to over five years).

Table 4.2
Children in different placement types

	Foster/Kin placements (n = 143)	Residential placements (n = 21)	Family placements (n = 16)
Average age when looked after*	7.5 yrs (sd 4.35)	11.8 yrs (sd 2.61)	0.2 yrs (sd 0.79)
Legal status when looked after**			
Care or Emergency Order	38%	19%	81%
Voluntarily accommodated	61%	71%	19%
Remanded/sentenced to care	1%	10%	0%
Previous period(s) in care***			
No	62%	43%	88%
Yes	38%	57%	12%
Average length of index care period****	10 months (sd 13.4)	18 months (sd 19.0)	6 months (sd 2.6)

* $F_{(2,179)} = 38.6$, p<0.001.
** $\chi^2 = 23.4$, $df = 4$, p < 0.001.
*** $\chi^2 = 7.6$, $df = 2$, p < 0.05.
**** $F_{(2,179)} = 4.7$, p<0.01.

[1]   Nine children in the case file sample were in the index care period for less than a month. These were children who were eligible for the sample because, although returned to their parents within six weeks of entering care, they had re-entered care within the same year (see Chapter 2).

Placement quality was variable. Nonetheless, over half of the children (53%) we interviewed described their time in foster care in positive terms and a few were clear that they would have liked to have stayed longer with their foster carers. Satisfaction with placements appeared to be about more than just good-quality care (although favouritism or inequalities in treatment were quickly picked up by the children). Being close to friends, liking the other children in the placement and being happy at school and in the locality were also important, as was the relationship between the foster carers and the child's family.

Contact with families

Contact with the children's parents was usually established quite quickly after the children started to be looked after. For a quarter (26%) it occurred within two days of entry to care and for a further third (35%) within a week or two. In situations where the family relationships were very strained, parties could need considerable space from each other, and sometimes contact did not start until a fortnight or more after the child entered care (see, for example, Abigail's story).

Abigail's story

Abigail's relationship with her mother was very volatile and Abigail, who was 12, frequently absconded from home and went to stay with friends. On two occasions when she refused to go home, children's services became involved and Abigail was accommodated. She told of violence within the family but a paediatrician's examination was inconclusive. However, Abigail then sustained an injury during a row with her mother and had to stay in hospital overnight. A child protection investigation (section 47 enquiry) was initiated, which resulted in a deterioration in Abigail's relationship with her mother and she was again accommodated (the study care period). Both mother and daughter stated that they wanted nothing more to do with each other. However, they began to speak on the phone two weeks later and

---

their relationship gradually improved. Abigail did not want to go home at that time, saying that it was hard living with her mother. Two weeks later, however, the pair had contact and reunification was planned. Both remained ambivalent about it but the case was closed very quickly after the return took place.

In a small number of cases the index care period signalled the complete breakdown of the children's relationship with the parent with whom they had been living and contact was instead instigated with the child's other parent once they had been located. Other reasons for a period without contact included the child being placed out of county, in a secure unit or residential school, or the parent disappearing or being hospitalised because of mental health or drug or alcohol problems. Where children had no face-to-face contact at all while the child was in care (5%), it was usually because the period in care was very short, the parents remained in prison or psychiatric hospital or the family relationships were very strained.

For two-fifths of the parents having contact, children's services departments (30%) or the courts (10%) imposed conditions with respect to the frequency of contact. Where conditions were imposed, the children were significantly younger (average age 5.5 years compared with average age 8.6 years where no conditions were imposed) and were more likely to have been subject to a child protection plan at some earlier point (68% compared with 43%). In many cases there was also a child protection investigation and in these circumstances children's services departments tended to take more control over planning the return and often supervised contact (86% compared with 40% where no contact restrictions were imposed).

Evolving arrangements for contact were made with parents whose circumstances changed frequently. New siblings were born into or joined a tenth of the households and just over a third of the children (36%) experienced at least one change of the adults in the household (a parent or partner leaving or arriving). Some supervised contact was held in contact centres or other children's services venues but often social workers tried to normalise it by meeting in the family home or the homes of carers or kin.

Some parents' lives, especially those with drug or alcohol problems, continued to be very chaotic (with some spiralling downhill once the children became looked after) and a tenth of the parents were thus very unreliable when it came to contact. The consistency of a further nine per cent was very variable but most parents (81%) adhered well to the contact arrangements, informing children's services or the caregiver if contact was not going to be possible. Support for contact was provided to most families (64%) in the form of transport or financial provision, but was not needed in just over a quarter of cases (27%) where parents or children managed the arrangements themselves. Children frequently took the bus or walked home after school once or twice a week or were taken there by foster carers or kin. For almost a tenth of families (9%), though, support for contact was needed but was not provided by children's services and in a few cases this contributed to contact unreliability.

For two-thirds of the children contact was meant to happen very regularly – twice weekly or more – but for others it was set at weekly intervals (16%), every two or three weeks (6%), or monthly or less (2%). For a tenth, the frequency of contact was very variable depending on parents' circumstances. Where the contact frequency was low (less then fortnightly), return home was not generally anticipated. Contact between siblings was less regulated and was often managed by foster carers or the young people themselves.

Before the children returned home, in most cases, the amount of contact the children had with their parents increased. Almost half of the children (47%) stayed home for two nights or more prior to their full-time return and a further quarter stayed overnight at least once. Others (12%) increased the frequency or duration of their day visits home in preparation for the return but for 16 per cent of the children there was no change in their contact frequency prior to the return. Most of these returns were unplanned with children absconding home from care or parents removing children without warning from voluntary care.

Descriptions of the quality of the contact for the children were very variable and in over a quarter of the cases (29%) it was not possible to ascertain the quality of the contact from the file. For two-fifths of the children (40%), contact was described in positive terms; for a quarter, the parent–child relationship was described as adequate; and in only six per cent of cases was the contact quality described as poor. In these cases there was ongoing antagonism between the parents and children or concerns about neglect or a lack of appropriate boundaries whilst the children were at home.

Abuse during contact

Contact was not always safe and eight children, to our knowledge, were abused by their parent or step-parent during contact and one by his brother. Six children were emotionally abused, two were slapped whilst at home and one boy was seen to be knocked to the floor and kicked and punched by his father because he had stolen money from him. Notwithstanding this incident, he returned home shortly after that.

Abuse in care

Nine children alleged abuse by their caregivers whilst they were looked after, including one allegation of inappropriate touching by a residential carer, five of hitting or aggressive restraint by foster or residential carers and three others (one alongside physical abuse) of name-calling or other forms of emotional abuse.

A further nine children experienced abuse at the hands of other children or other adults whilst they were in care. Children in residential care were particularly at risk of experiencing emotional, physical or sexual abuse from other children in the placement or from predatory adults. One girl was sexually assaulted by a fellow resident in a children's home while being held down by another. Others were coerced into sexual activity sometimes by members of the same sex and in one case by a paedophile who picked up the boy outside his children's home. School could also be a setting for adverse experiences and two children were the victims of racial harassment at school, with several more experiencing bullying. In total for 26 children (14%) experiences of abuse did not stop once they were in care. Eleven experienced emotional abuse, six physical abuse, five sexual abuse, and four multiple forms of abuse.

We turn now to consider the parents' and children's views of this period in care.

The parents' views of the children's care experiences

The parents who were interviewed had a range of views about their children's time in care. Two-thirds were broadly positive about the care their children had experienced but a third were much less happy about it. Of the 25 children who had been in foster care, three-quarters of the parents were positive about it, whereas in relation to the young people (8) who had been in residential care, only half of the parents were positive. Fourteen of the 34 parents whom we interviewed (44%) reported no change in their children's behaviour whilst they were in care, eight considered that their behaviour had worsened, five said that their behaviour had been mixed, and only five (16%) had seen an improvement. On the other hand, three-fifths (21) of the parents thought that the foster carers or residential workers had actively encouraged or helped towards the children's return.

The parents who were positive about the experience of care

These parents were often enthusiastic in their praise of foster carers, saying that they had been "fantastic" and "superb". One mother spoke for many when she said of the foster carers:

They were great – lovely people... She became a lovely friend over the couple of months.

Parents expressed appreciation for foster carers who had given their children structure, boundaries, one-to-one attention, stability, routines or discipline and who had arranged outings and activities for them or had made efforts to maintain a pre-schooler in her playgroup. Parents were particularly positive about foster carers with whom they had made good personal relationships. They were especially grateful when foster carers had reassured them that they saw them as capable and were hoping their children would be returned to them. This was important because a few mothers had feared that they would never see their children again or that the children would never understand why their parents had left them in care. One mother said of the foster carers:

> *[They] suggested to me different things. You know they'd actually listen to me, how I felt and what I wanted, you know, and what she needed and stuff like that.*

These foster carers had suggested that the mother should not ring her daughter daily and should put down the telephone and not take her out when she was poorly behaved. The mother said that it was 'nice to be told' by people who were 'on my level' and who praised her and said she was a loving mother. The mother said that her daughter 'loves them to bits' and still wrote to the foster carers, who had retained an interest in her. One young mother who had been in a mother and baby foster placement said of the foster carer:

> *She was my second mum . . . I loved her to bits.*

One mother who had a poor bond with her daughter appreciated the care that her child had received and the improvement in her behaviour. She explained that she had found difficult the fact that her daughter Shameem loved the foster mother and was so close to her, while at the same time feeling relieved that she was in care and a weight had been taken off her shoulders. This mother also mentioned that she had felt guilty when her daughter went into care and that Shameem had 'felt like I'd rejected and abandoned her'. At that time the mother felt that she 'wasn't being the parent I wanted to be' and became depressed. Another mother was honest in considering that perhaps her daughter had needed to get away from her for a while. A few parents were relieved that their children had been diagnosed as having a specific difficulty while being looked after, like the mother whose son was diagnosed as having ADD and put on medication whilst in foster care.

Parents were sometimes also fulsome in their praise of residential workers, describing them as "brilliant" even when, in more than one case, the children's behaviour had worsened under the influence of other residents. One mother was reassured when the children's home where her son was placed reported the same behaviour as she had experienced. Parents sometimes saw the discipline in a children's home as good. In addition, one mother reported that entry to care had made her son see that 'the grass was not always greener on the other side'.

A mother, whose son Phil had spend a year in a secure unit after a serious offence, had been pleased with the help he had received while there. He had been treated by a psychiatrist and psychologist, so that he came to understand his problems and their impact on the family and could also control his temper better. She explained that the treatment had:

> Taught him how to channel his anger and his frustration into other avenues.

Phil would go to his room when angry and he had responded well to the behaviour modification system in the unit. His mother was told that she should have had help long before, which helped to counteract her feelings of failure as a parent.

The parents who were negative about the experience of care

Whilst the majority of parents were positive about the care their children had received when they were being looked after, a third were much more negative. A common complaint with adolescents and pre-teens who went into residential units was that their behaviour actually worsened, partly because discipline was not strict enough (see also Fisher et al, 1986) and partly because of the influence of other resident children (see also Sinclair and Gibbs, 1998; Farmer and Pollock, 1998). For example, Nona's mother, Mrs Benton, said that the children went out at night from their residential unit and got into stolen cars with boys and that if they did not return, residential staff would inform the police but not the parents. Mrs Benton had found her teenage daughter high on drugs with a group of children in a house. Later, the children's home 'packed her bags' and threw her out. The mother thought:

> Right now you've made her worse, you don't want her either.

Mr and Mrs Benton felt that social workers blamed them for their daughter's behaviour but saw the school as very understanding.

Another group of parents was unhappy about the quality of care provided, which, as we saw earlier in this chapter, in a few cases had failed to keep children safe. One mother felt that the independent children's home where her son Ross was accommodated had 'shut the family out', had not worked towards reunion with her because they depended on the income from fees, and had failed to provide Ross with an adequate education. A few (5) of the parents whom we interviewed had removed children from their placements, including in two cases after an incident of abuse by another resident.

Seven mothers thought that foster care had not worked out for their children, sometimes because the children had not liked the foster carers, or had not settled in the placement or had wanted to come home. One mother, although relieved that her daughter was in care, was nonetheless angry that new things were bought for her daughter which, to the mother, seemed like a reward for her bad behaviour.

Two parents commented that their children had had many moves in care:

This all comes down to he's been into so many different placements.

Can't be good can it? I can't see how it could be good being moved from place to place.

The parents' views about contact before the children returned

As we have seen, levels of contact varied enormously. We were interested to know how satisfied parents were with the frequency of their contact whilst their children were being looked after. Where this was relevant, 16 parents (57%) said that it had been about the right amount, 11 (39%) that it had not been enough, and one mother considered that she had had too much contact. Twenty-one parents mentioned some difficulty with contact, including difficulties with supervised contact, contact restrictions, the children's behaviour, transport, the setting, the parents' own circumstances and combinations of these difficulties.

Two mothers described supervised contact as "intimidating" or "daunting". One mother found the family support worker's supervision of contact to be supportive, although she was unhappy about the restrictions on what she could say to her children during contact:

> *Things with social services were hard. And I wanted her home and the way they say is you're never allowed to tell your child that you want them home ... I'm allowed to tell them I miss them. I'm not allowed to cry in front of them ... because it disturbs them ... It is very, very hard. Because ... I want them to know that I still want them, that I want them home ... it left both me and Robyn very confused ... and that left the relationship very strained as well.*

Her views were echoed by another mother who said that 'there were lots of things I was not allowed to say' during contact. (In both these cases a decision had been taken that the children would remain in long-term care.) Another mother said that contact with her daughter had been supervised by the foster carers and that although she had been "disgusted" at first, she had soon found that they made her welcome.

Two mothers with small babies were allowed to feed and change them under the watchful eye of the foster mothers. One of them appreciated the fact that the foster mother involved her in visits to the GP and kept her fully informed if the baby was unwell. The other mother described her contact with her six-month-old baby, Nick, in this way:

Mother   *I found it difficult at first that I couldn't do certain things. You know, change his nappy and put him in the bath and things. But then after a while, obviously once [the foster carers] got to know me, I could. I could do my normal routine. When I came round she would step aside and I would do everything for him. So he could learn again that I was his mum and she wasn't.*

Interviewer *Would you say that the bond did build with Nick?*

Mother   *I'm not sure to be quite honest ... He would learn so much off them and nothing off me ... So I think he didn't really bond very much with me in that time at all.*

Contact with some children was fraught (see also Moyers *et al*, 2006) and a few children continued to show behavioural difficulties during contact. For example, one 10-year-old girl shunned her mother on visits, leaving her in tears. Six-year-old Jackie visited her mother three times a week. These visits would go alright until it was time for Jackie to return to care when she would get very angry and smash up her bedroom. Similarly, another mother described contact as an 'emotional rollercoaster' in which Robyn was delighted to be home and then 'gutted to leave'.

Five of the parents we interviewed did not want to see their children whilst they were looked after, either because they were exhausted by their difficult behaviour or because of a rift in their relationships before they went into care. Whilst some of the children felt the same way, others were less equable about the situation. Young people sometimes managed such situations by speaking regularly on the telephone to their parents. One mother went to live abroad for some time where she lost touch, although she did have increased contact after her return.

Several parents mentioned that social workers or occasionally relatives had provided transport for them to go to see their children. Carrie, a 13-year-old, had contact twice a week after school and stayed overnight on some weekends. In addition, the foster carer would take her to her mother's house each morning so that she could walk with her to school and Carrie would drop in on her family daily after school on her own initiative. Carrie felt that there was too little contact but her mother considered it was too much, as she wanted to get more of a break from the daughter she had been unable to control. Two other young people would also drop in regularly from school to see their mothers.

The children's views of their care experiences

Entering care

When asked how they had felt about going into care, the 19 young people whom we interviewed described feeling sad or upset (5), worried, anxious or scared (3), whilst the remainder told us that they had felt surprised, confused, rejected and abandoned, angry or relieved.

Three of the young people did not know why they had gone into care, but five explained that it had been because of a parent's hospitalisation, imprisonment, substance misuse or stress. Six children acknowledged that the difficulties had been in their own behaviour, whilst five said the problems had been in the parent–child relationship. Those young people who recognised their part in the need for admission to care sometimes described their behaviour at the time:

I kept running away and attacking my mum and I kept playing up. [Girl aged 9 when she entered care]

I've got ADHD. I was way beyond control . . . I was a cow, to be honest. [Girl aged 13 when she entered care]

I had lots of tantrums. Locked Mum and my brother out of the house. I was smashing things up, throwing ornaments. [Boy aged 12 when he entered care]

Some young people explained why they had behaved as they did or gave details about difficult relationships with parents or step-parents:

I didn't like my mum's [new] husband . . . So I tried to kill myself. Mum couldn't cope or didn't want me . . . I couldn't handle it. [Girl aged 13 when she entered care]

Mum couldn't cope with me – just about everything about me. [Boy aged 15 when he entered care]

One girl who had been singled out for rejection by her mother had felt pushed out of the family when she entered care and could not understand why her sister could remain at home when she could not.

Some of the children described their shock at discovering that they were going into care. One boy, who was 11 when he was accommodated, did not know why this had happened. He said:

It was just a sudden moment that I was took.

However, he did acknowledge that his behaviour at school had been difficult:

I felt angry and just couldn't hold it in any longer.

Another girl described the lack of notice she had received about her impending move:

I never knew I was going there . . . I went to school one day . . . I met the social services after school and they told me that they was moving me.

Similarly, a boy who had not understood why he went into care said:

'Cos they just took me and I didn't know anything what was happening or anything. Bit scary.

Two young people explained that they had coped with care because of either their own or their siblings' prior experience of care. Jardine, who had been accommodated at the age of 12 when her mother was imprisoned for supplying drugs, said:

It didn't really bother me because all my sisters and brothers have been in care.

Jason, who was 14 when he went into care, explained that it was:

OK to go into care because I had been in several times before . . . I could get out, clear my head.

Being in care

The young people reported a range of feelings about being in care. Five had felt happy or excited in the main, but five others had been angry, upset or anxious; three remembered how lonely they had felt; two recalled their feelings of rejection and three their confused or mixed feelings. When asked about their secondary feelings about the situation, another four reported feeling happy or relieved to be in care, although nine others described anxiety, loneliness and feeling upset. One girl, who was 13 when she went to foster carers, said:

I didn't want to go in at first . . . and it was alright when I went in there 'cos I had pocket money and everything.

Another, who was 10 when she joined her foster family, said:

I knew I'd be treated OK but I'd rather live with my mother if I could ... I was so upset because I couldn't live with my mum but Jenny [the foster carer] made me feel welcome.

Some reported very positive experiences of care once they were there. For example, Tina said that she loved her foster carers and Leo said that it was 'great fun' with his. Sheila, who had not been happy at home, said:

I fitted in with the rest of the family. I look at her [the foster carer] as a mum ... I would have rather stayed there until I was going to leave care.

However, a few had been less happy in care. For example, Carrie described having to force down meals at the foster carers' because she did not like them and missing her family very much. Nonetheless, she acknowledged that she had got on much better with her mother when she was not living with her. Another young person complained that he had not been allowed out much and felt as if he had been locked up.

Several children described a number of moves in care, with one girl saying she had lived with 'loads of people' whilst looked after and a boy saying:

I was just a bit confused and a bit scared that I was just put somewhere different. 'Cos I didn't know anything then.

The children's views of contact

Eight of the 19 children interviewed said that they had had the right amount of contact with family members whilst in care, although eight thought that they had had too little. All but three of those who had had contact had enjoyed it most of the time, although one child described feeling upset when contact visits ended. Another young person said:

[I was] happy that I actually knew they [the family] were alright.

A few children who were in children's homes explained that contact had been held out in placements as a reward for good behaviour or withheld if they had misbehaved or run away (see also Farmer and Parker, 1991).

The social workers' views of contact

The social workers' knowledge about the children's contact was variable, especially since arrangements in most cases had been complex and the frequency and quality of contact had sometimes been inconsistent. Nonetheless, in some cases overnight and weekend stays were seen as providing social workers with an indication of what would be needed to support the return home, for example, the provision of respite care.

Occasionally, a parent's contact with their child had undermined their placement in care, such as in Suzie's case where, although face-to-face contact was supervised, her mother rang her daily, using emotional blackmail and encouraging her to return home, so that a series of placements were undermined and Suzie oscillated between care and home. No way had been found to control these telephone calls.

Now that we have considered how children fared whilst in care and parents' and children's experiences of care, in the following chapter we examine planning for return.

Summary

- The reasons for children becoming looked after were parental problems, parent–child relationship breakdown, concerns about abuse or neglect and, more rarely, the child's difficult behaviour.
- Children were most often voluntarily accommodated (59%), but a fifth were removed under emergency orders and a further fifth under interim or full care orders. Children removed in emergency situations or under care orders were significantly younger than those voluntarily accommodated.
- Most children (79%) then returned home from foster or kinship care settings, but 13 per cent did so from residential settings and 8 per cent from mother and baby foster placements or residential family assessment centres. The average length of the index care period for all the children was 10.3 months.

- Most children (82%) saw their parents weekly or more often and most, but not all, parents complied well with the contact arrangements. Two-fifths of the parents were subject to contact conditions. Some mothers described supervised contact as intimidating and daunting.
- Prior to their return home, most children (84%) had increased contact with their parents, including overnight stays for almost three-quarters.
- Twenty-six children (14%) alleged abuse by their caregivers, other children or adults whilst were looked after or alleged abuse during contact.

Parent, child and social worker perspectives on the index care period

- Of the 34 parents interviewed, only five (16%) saw an improvement in their children's behaviour whilst they were looked after, five (16%) said that their behaviour had been mixed, 44 per cent reported no change and eight (25%) considered that their behaviour had worsened. Two-thirds were broadly positive about the care their children had experienced but a third were much less happy about it. Parents were considerably more positive about foster care than about residential placements.
- Almost two-thirds of the parents thought foster carers or residential workers had actively encouraged or helped towards the children's return. Parents were particularly positive about foster carers with whom they had made good personal relationships. They were grateful when foster carers had reassured parents that they saw them as capable.
- Amongst the third of parents who were more negative, a common complaint was that the behaviour of adolescents who went into residential units actually worsened, partly because discipline was not strict enough and partly because of the influence of other resident children. Five of the 34 parents who were interviewed had removed children from their placements because of concerns about their safety.
- Twenty-one parents mentioned some difficulty with contact, including difficulties with supervised contact, contact restrictions and the children's behaviour.

- Some of the children had had little notice that they were going to be looked after and had been shocked when they went away. They often felt sad, upset and anxious. Those who had been in care previously or whose siblings had been looked after felt better prepared to face it.
- After the initial uncertainties, children were often positive about their placements, especially those in foster care. Those who had had placement moves had often found this difficult.
- Of the 19 children interviewed who had had contact, half thought it had been the right amount and half had wanted more.

5 Planning for the children's returns

In this chapter we examine social work planning whilst the children were in care, and the involvement of the courts and other agencies in assessing and planning for return. We note whether conditions were specified for the parents and/or children in order to achieve reunification and the work that was conducted with families in preparation for the return.

The children's ages at return

In order to provide a context for understanding the care planning that took place, we look ahead first to how old the children were when they returned to their parent/s. By that time, 30 per cent of the children were under five, 21 per cent were aged between five and ten and half (49%) were aged between 10 and 14.

The initial care plans for the children

For the largest group of children (45%) the first recorded plan was "time-limited assessment", with "return home" the initial plan for only slightly fewer (41%). For a small proportion of children (8%), return home had originally been ruled out altogether and other permanence plans had been made instead. For a few children (6%), who had all returned home within two months, no clear plans had been recorded whilst they were in care. Most of them had absconded home soon after entering care; some had been removed from their placements by their parents or had returned after their parents were discharged after a brief period in hospital or police custody.

Children's legal status, their age at entry to care, and their previous child protection and care history were all significantly related to children's initial care plans as was the length of their time in care (see Table 5.1).

The children who returned home before there had been time to make a plan for them stayed in care very briefly. They tended to be older when they came into care (average age almost 11 years); to have been in care (91%) and returned home a number of times already; and at some stage

Table 5.1
Factors related to children's initial care plans

		No clear plan (n = 11)	Return home (n = 74)	Time-limited assessment (n = 81)	Other permanence plan (n = 14)
Mean age at entry to care*		10.7 yrs (sd 3.03)	8.3 yrs (sd 4.76)	5.8 yrs (sd 4.71)	8.4 yrs (sd 3.41)
Age range at entry to care (95% CI for mean)		8.7–12.7	7.2–9.4	4.7–6.9	6.4–10.4
Legal status**					
Emergency or care order		45%	20%	54%	50%
Voluntarily accommodated		45%	78%	44%	50%
Remanded to care		10%	2%	2%	–
Ever subject to a child protection (CP) plan***	Yes	82%	38%	57%	79%
	No	18%	62%	43%	21%
Previously looked after****	Yes	91%	43%	28%	28%
	No	9%	57%	72%	72%
Mean no. of previous returns#		1.9 (sd 1.1)	0.81 (sd 1.4)	0.36 (sd 0.6)	0.57 (sd 1.01)
Mean time looked after##		0.4 mnths (sd 0.68)	6.8 mnths (sd 9.49)	10.9 mnths (sd 13.44)	32.8 mnths (sd 19.08)

* $F_{(3,179)} = 6.4$, p<0.001; **$\chi2 = 24.1$, $df = 6$, $p < 0.001$; ***$\chi2 = 14.1$, $df = 3$, $p < 0.01$; ****$\chi2 = 17.6$, $df = 3$, $p < 0.001$;
# $F_{(3,179)} = 8.8$, p<0.001; ## $F_{(3,179)} = 20.6$, p<0.001.

to have been subject to a child protection plan (82%). They entered care by a number of routes: under emergency orders (45%) or by being voluntarily accommodated (45%) or remanded to care (10%). It is worth noting that there was least planning and oversight for this most problematic group of children, although the sudden nature of their returns made planning difficult.

Children for whom return home was the initial plan were on average aged just over eight at entry to care and stayed there for just over six-and-a-half months. For over half (57%) this was their first time in care and most were accommodated (78%) and had not previously been subject to a child protection plan (62%). They were not generally considered to be problematic cases, although a good number of them had already experienced one or more failed returns home. Yet, in spite of this, another return was planned.

In contrast, many of the children for whom a period of time-limited assessment was the plan had been taken into police protection or entered care on orders (54%), having previously been subject to a child protection plan (57%). These were younger children, with an average age of 5.8 years and most had spent almost 11 months in care before they went home. Most had not been in care before (72%), although concerns had been rising about several. As would be expected, most of the children placed with their parents in family assessment centres had this initial plan.

Not surprisingly, children whose initial plans were adoption or long-term care generally came from families where there had been serious child protection concerns (79% of this group had previously been subject to a child protection plan). One family had been convicted of child cruelty, others had histories of abuse or neglect. For one baby and two young siblings coming from such backgrounds, adoption was thought to be in the children's best interests. Permanence plans away from their parents had been made because the children were not considered to be safe at home or were beyond their parents' control. However, these plans were not fulfilled, so children returned after long periods away (an average of nearly three years). These children were of a similar age to those in the return home group when they entered care (average age 8.4 years).

Assessment

Domestic violence, parental substance misuse, parental learning difficulties or mental health problems were not significantly related to which kind of care plan was made. In contrast, assessment activity did vary in relation to these initial care plans. Although a quarter of the children with time-limited assessment plans were never actually assessed, a comprehensive assessment of the children's circumstances was significantly more likely to occur with this initial plan than any other. A third (36%) of the children with other permanence plans and over half (55%) of the children with plans for return home were reunified without any assessment of their family situation. This in part reflected the number of cases where the decision for the return was taken in the context of care proceedings. The courts were involved in this way in the returns of almost two-fifths of the time-limited assessment cases (38%), but in only a few of the cases with other permanence plans (14%) or a plan for return home (7%). In total the courts were directly involved in this way in a fifth (21%) of the cases

In most of the cases with such direct court involvement, comprehensive assessments of the child and family were arranged to assist the court's decision-making (see Table 5.2). In most cases (58%), more than one type of assessment was undertaken, usually a core assessment alongside a psychological or other expert assessment. In others, only core assessments (11%) or expert assessments (26%) were found on file and, in a small number of cases (5%), a residential assessment was undertaken.

Outside the court arena, fuller assessments (that is not just an initial assessment) were completed three-fifths of the time when the child's initial care plan was time-limited assessment (60%) or long-term foster or residential care (58%), but only two-fifths (40%) of the time where the initial plan was return home. In these circumstances there were fewer expert assessments (11%) and multiple assessments (20%), but a greater use of parenting assessments, which were usually conducted at the local family centre.

In total, of the 180 children, over two-fifths (43%) returned home without any assessment of their situation or after only an initial assessment had been conducted. Lewis' story describes one such return.

Table 5.2

The relationship between assessment and whether the return took place within care proceedings

	Court involved (n = 38)	*Court not involved (n = 142)*	*All children (n = 180)*
No assessment	0%	44%	35%
Initial assessment only	0%	10%	8%
Core assessment only	11%	11%	11%
Expert assessment (e.g. psychological)	26%	11%	14%
Residential assessment	5%	1%	2%
Other assessment (e.g. parenting)	0%	3%	3%
More than one of above	58%	20%	27%
Total	**100%**	**100%**	**100%**

Lewis' story

There were concerns about the care of Lewis as a baby and the case went to court. Custody was awarded to Lewis' father and contact with his mother prohibited. At the age of 12, Lewis moved from his father to live with his mother. She had problems with alcohol and had violent relationships. There were immediate concerns that she was drinking heavily and abusing Lewis and he spent a month in care before returning to his father. However, later that year Lewis was remanded in custody for offending. At his father's request he was again placed in care. Despite the court order prohibiting contact and Lewis' express desire not to live with his mother, it was quickly decided that he would return to her. A few days later, without any assessment, he moved to live with his mother. This was the study return and it lasted only a few days until Lewis was arrested and was remanded to the care of the local authority.

Of the cases where assessments were undertaken, core assessments were completed for just over a quarter (27%) of the children (11% alone and 16% alongside another form of assessment), whilst assessments by mental health professionals featured in almost two-fifths of cases (37%). Residential assessments were completed for almost a tenth of the children and parenting or other types of assessment (for example, independent social worker assessments) for 13 per cent.

Much of this assessment (43%) was multi-agency, especially when the returns took place within care proceedings. Only a third of all the assessments were conducted solely by children's services and a quarter by other agencies.

Researcher ratings of the value of these assessments found that, whilst half of the assessments had been sufficiently analytical and adequately assessed all of the risks to the child such that they had been a useful basis on which to make the return decision, the other half had been only partially useful (47%) or not really useful (2%). Only a third of the assessments conducted by children's services alone and only two-fifths by another agency alone were thought to have been fully analytical and useful, as compared with almost three-quarters of those completed by both children's services and other agencies (see Table 5.3). This is not a reflection of the competence of either social workers or other professionals, but highlights the importance of multi-agency assessment for families with multiple or complex problems (see also, for example, Kendall *et al*, 2010).

Where multi-agency assessments were conducted, children were more

Table 5.3
Usefulness of the assessments conducted

	Children's services (n = 40)	Other agency (n = 27)	Both (n = 50)	Total (n = 117)
Not useful	5%	–	–	2%
Partially useful	62%	59%	28%	47%
Fully useful	33%	41%	72%	51%
Total	**100%**	**100%**	**100%**	**100%**

Table 5.4
How well problems were addressed prior to return

	No assessment (n = 63)	Children's services assessment (n = 40)	Other agency assessment (n = 27)	Both (n = 50)	Total (n = 180)
No problems addressed	46%	18%	7%	2%	22%
Some problems addressed	41%	52%	67%	58%	52%
All problems addressed	13%	30%	26%	40%	26%
Total	**100%**	**100%**	**100%**	**100%**	**100%**

likely to be returned home safely. In most (98%) of such cases, researcher ratings indicated that some or all of the problems that had led to the children entering care had received attention. This included 40 per cent where all the major problems had been adequately addressed (see Table 5.4). This latter figure is still quite low because, although assessment was linked to service provision, as we shall see later in this chapter, the work was not always completed (due to resource shortages, missed appointments or the children going home prematurely) or was not successful.

Where children's services or another agency alone conducted the assessment, all of the problems that had led to the children entering care had only been adequately addressed (such that the returns could safely be undertaken) in 30 per cent and 26 per cent of the cases respectively, and this figure fell to 13 per cent where no assessments had been carried out. Worryingly, almost half of this latter group of children (46%) returned home without anything having changed at all. Examples of returns where all the problems had been addressed included a mother with mental health problems who was stabilised on medication, discharged from psychiatric hospital and then regularly monitored or a mother living with domestic violence who asked her abusive partner to leave the family home and ended the relationship.

However, in many cases, whilst the primary presenting problems might have been resolved before children returned home, important underlying issues remained undetected or untreated and subsequently threatened the stability of the returns. Indeed, one or more issues remained unresolved in almost three-quarters of the cases (74%).

Professional support in preparation for the return

Professional support could be key to the stability of the returns and was more likely to occur following assessment. We considered specialist support from children's services to have been given when services were provided at a family centre or other venue, as opposed to routine support or direct work conducted by the social worker. After assessment, two-thirds (65%) of the parents and over half (55%) of the children received such specialist support from either children's services or another agency prior to the return, compared with only a third of parents (33%) and children (36%) whose circumstances had not been assessed.

Some of the other parents (20%) and children (9%) had been referred to mental health or other professionals before the return, but did not appear to have received a service. Sometimes this was because they failed to turn up for any of the appointments (45% of referred parents and 22% of referred children), but more often it was because the service was not available in time or the outcome of the referral was not clear from the file (55% of referred parents and 78% of children). Nonetheless, mental health or other professionals saw a third (34%) of the 180 children and half (49%) of their parents at this stage (see Table 5.5).

Much of the work with parents concentrated on the parents' own difficult circumstances or experience of adversity (37%) or their parenting abilities (21%), whilst work with children tended to focus on their behaviour (24%) or experiences of abuse (12%). For a quarter of the parents and a third of the children, the work had multiple strands to it, whilst for others the purpose of the work was not clear from the file.

Social workers also conducted direct work with a fifth of the parents (22%) and children (19%), many of whom were also receiving support from other professionals. This work tended to focus on parenting skills, behaviour management and protection from harm.

Table 5.5
Support in preparation for the return

	Parents			**Children**		
	Assess-ment	*no assess-ment*	**Total**	*Assess-ment*	*no assess-ment*	**Total**
Professional support	65%	33%	**49%**	55%	36%	**34%**
Social worker support	23%	21%	**22%**	32%	20%	**19%**

No work was completed with any family member by either social workers or other professionals in almost a quarter of the cases (23%). This occurred significantly more frequently where there had been no assessment of the family circumstances. Where no work was undertaken with any family member, problems tended to persist into the return.

Researcher ratings indicated that in over two-fifths of the cases (44%) where no work was conducted, none of the problems that had led to the children entering care had been addressed. This compares with only 14 per cent of cases where work had been completed with either the parent or child or both.

Conditions for return

In some situations the social worker would require not only that work had been undertaken but that specific improvements were seen before the children could be returned home. Conditions such as these were set in just over a third of cases (37%) and were more likely to feature after the family situation had been assessed, where the initial plan was time-limited assessment or return home and when returns occurred in the context of care proceedings. All these findings were significant.

The conditions generally aimed to improve the child's safety, for example, by requiring that an abusive partner leave the family home; that parents reduce, control or abstain from drug or alcohol use; that parents with mental health conditions seek treatment or take prescription medication and/or that home conditions or parenting standards improve.

In half of these cases (49%) the conditions were specified in a formal written agreement signed by the parent/s. It is quite possible that further cases were subject to conditions but that these were agreed verbally with the social worker and not recorded on file.

The presence of conditions was linked to service provision, with four-fifths (81%) of the parents receiving specialist or social work support to assist them to meet the conditions, compared with under half (46%) of parents where conditions were not set. However, only a fifth of the agreements (whether formalised or not) specified a clear timescale in which the changes needed to take place and only two-fifths clearly spelled out the consequences for the parents of failing to make the required changes.

Nevertheless, setting conditions (and providing the services to achieve them) appeared to be a successful way of encouraging change and by the time of the return, almost three-fifths of the children's parents had met all of the conditions specified. A further quarter had met most or some of the conditions and only a small number (17%) had achieved few or none of the necessary changes.

Conditions were also set for a very small number of children (5%) and mostly focused on improvements in their behaviour. They tended to be contracts setting out what was and was not acceptable behaviour at home. All but one of these agreements were accompanied by specialist or social work support.

The parents' views of assessment prior to return

Just over half of the parents who were interviewed said that either they or their children had been assessed prior to the return. For example, Shameem returned to her mother on the recommendation of the children's guardian. The guardian conducted a family assessment, a child psychiatrist and a psychologist assessed Shameem, whilst a drugs expert assessed the mother who had difficulties with depression and drugs misuse. Another mother with mental health problems, who had misused drugs, was an in-patient in a psychiatric hospital while her daughter was looked after and she recalled an assessment at which she was given certain things she would have to do in order for her daughter to be returned.

Parents who went to a residential assessment or mother and baby foster placements also underwent assessments of their ability to care for their young children, and in the latter situation foster carers took part in these assessments. When a child had been removed because of an injury, the parent to whom return was planned would be carefully assessed, sometimes at a family centre. In one such case, two social workers and a social work assistant visited the mother four or five times a week to conduct an assessment of whether it was safe to return a toddler to a mother who had physically abused her older brother. The mother felt that at first 'the social workers tried to dig the dirt' on her but that they later worked towards the child returning, as did the foster carers.

It was less clear how often older children with emotional and behavioural difficulties had been assessed. John, who was beyond the control of his parents, was assessed by his social worker and a psychiatrist but the parents said that they had not found these assessments useful. Guy was a boy of 14 who absconded to his mother from his foster carers. The social worker assessed the home as satisfactory, but the mother said in interview that they had thought she was coping when she was not.

A small number of these children were assessed by a child psychiatrist. In one such case, the psychiatrist assessed a 10-year-old girl as having a conduct and attachment disorder, and it was noted that the mother was not responding to intervention so that reunification was ruled out. However, this girl did go home because her mother removed her from her children's home.

Some children were returned to their parents without an adequate assessment having been made and therefore without any changes having taken place in either the children or the parents. In one such case, Josie, who was an aggressive and angry nine-year-old, returned to her parents after ten months in care but without an assessment or any improvement in her or her parents. Her difficult behaviour resumed once she was home and the return broke down. Another child who was violent and aggressive returned to his parents at the age of nine after difficulties in his children's home. Without assessment or intervention during his time in care, the return failed after his violent behaviour flared up again. In addition, in a number of cases, a parent's substance misuse problem had not been assessed or treated and the return of their children was short lived.

The parents' views on conditions for return

Whilst the use of formal written agreements was infrequent in the interview sample, a number of the parents we interviewed were clear that there were conditions attached to their children's return. In five cases, the conditions related to excluding the other parent. For example, one mother knew that the father was not to see the child, except during supervised contact; two other mothers knew that they were not to resume relationships with their partners; and one father was told that he had to be at home whenever the children were there because the mother was not capable of parenting the children because of her alcohol problem.

Other conditions related to the parents' care. One mother had signed a written agreement that she would not neglect or harm her child, because she had physically abused her first child. Another mother was clear that, having completed six months of treatment, she had to remain sober and this was supervised. Yet another mother had to attend a family centre once a week, seek counselling through her GP and see a family support worker at home, who worked with her on maintaining boundaries and on her parenting skills. She was clear that she was not allowed to miss the family centre visits. She said:

Because it was enforced, it made me hate it even more.

In only one case in the interview sample were conditions set for a young person. A young man who returned on one year's licence from a secure unit, with conditions about his actions, knew that if he broke the terms of the licence he would have to return to the unit.

The parents' views on interventions while the children were in care

The parents' experience of social workers

Twenty of the parents interviewed (59%) considered that their social worker had worked actively towards the children returning to their care. Ten parents (29%) thought that the social worker had not done so, whilst four reported that some of the social workers involved with them had done so and others had not. The parents appreciated social workers who had worked actively to get their children returned to them.

Some parents had a high regard for social workers whom they saw as helpful. For example, one mother said:

> *Wilma Green was brilliant, absolutely wonderful. She's the best social worker Ross could ever have had.*

Other social workers were praised for helping find parents housing to enable them to leave mother and baby foster placements and a few had discussed with the parents how to deal with their difficulties if they arose again.

On the other hand, one mother had not seen her social worker whilst her daughter was in care and three parents had had real difficulties with their social workers and were only able to work with children's services after a new worker was allocated.

It was not uncommon for parents to say that they had wanted help for their children, and sometimes help to manage them, but that social workers had not known what to do about children with behavioural and emotional difficulties. Certainly, as we have seen, the parents quite often spoke of knowing that their children had serious problems from a young age and attempting unsuccessfully to get them assessed and to receive help for them. For example, one mother said:

> *I just wanted someone to help me and like I told them before, when he was younger I needed help and they used to keep saying to me 'Oh, you can cope. He's OK.' And I knew there was something wrong with him.*

It is true that whilst substitute care had provided some space between the children and their parents, quite often no work had been conducted with the child or parent on the difficulties underlying their problems.

On the other hand, some parents actively resisted the help that was provided. For example, one mother had had to do a child management course in order for her daughter to be returned to her, but she had regarded the course as "silly".

Parents were critical of social workers who were not firm with their adolescent children and did not confront them with their poor behaviour. They saw it as inappropriate when a social worker took a child out for a meal at McDonald's after a bout of bad behaviour, thus appearing to reward even quite severe oppositional behaviour. One father said:

There's this culture of 'the child is always right' . . . and it ain't true.

In contrast, they were appreciative of social workers who did not provide treats during periods of difficult behaviour, dealt with adolescents as 'unruly stroppy teenagers' when this was appropriate, and who listened to the parents as well as to the children.

Some felt that social workers lacked experience:

It's all bookwork . . . they've just no kids of their own. They've got no experience, no life.

Parents' views of review meetings

Some parents said that social workers did not listen to their views at meetings and some felt more generally that social workers did not listen to them. Others described feeling daunted by the size of review meetings or had not found statutory reviews helpful:

You can't tell social workers anything because they already know how you feel.

[At meetings] They just talk around you... you're not allowed to express your views.

One mother reported that at a child protection review at which the father was present, she was asked if he was still violent to her and felt constrained to deny it for fear of reprisals from him. One couple described reviews as:

It was at the social services when they all get together in a huddle and sit at one end of the table and try and put you at the other and talk down at you.

In this case the social worker wanted their son to return before the parents felt ready, as they were requesting help for him and for themselves prior to reunification.

The parents' views of assistance from other professionals whilst the children were looked after

Two sets of parents mentioned that their teenage children had had a mentor during their time in care, that the young people had been able to talk to them and that this had been useful. Two children had been assisted by youth offending team workers, about whom parents were also positive.

The boy who had been in a secure unit had regular sessions with a child psychiatrist and a clinical psychologist while in the unit, which as we have seen, had helped him a great deal. A six-year-old girl who had been looked after for over two years had behaviour therapy at a child psychiatric unit and three years of play therapy. However, her mother considered that these had been 'the wrong kind of help'. A few children had been given help with anger management, although parents had not generally seen this as bringing about much change.

One teenage girl, Tina, was looked after because of her frequent suicide threats. Child and Adolescent Mental Health Services (CAMHS) provided sessions for Tina and her mother individually and together, which proved beneficial. Her mother said:

> I learned that part of Tina's problem was my past . . . which seemed very very daft . . . it was scary, you know, to go back into your past and bring things up that would affect your children . . . And it did help, although it was horrible having to go back.

A second mother had received weekly visits from a specialist substance misuse worker and treatment over three months by a clinical psychologist, which she had found very helpful. Other helpful interventions included: professionals from a residential unit having regular meetings with a boy's parents and doing some work with them after he was discharged and therapeutic work while a couple were in a residential family assessment unit, coupled with discussion with their social worker about how to deal with their difficulties. However, one couple had found family therapy to try to help them establish appropriate boundaries with their adolescent daughter less helpful than a psychiatric nurse's assessment of their daughter.

The social workers' views of assessment

The social workers explained that when no formal assessment had been undertaken prior to the child's return home, this was generally because the family was already known to children's services so an assessment was not considered necessary. This included a case where the child had been removed from his foster placement by a step-parent with a history of abuse to this boy, where it appeared that an assessment would have been beneficial. In addition, with the benefit of hindsight, some practitioners considered that where there had been no assessment, children had sometimes entered care when they should not have done so and remained in care thereafter longer than was necessary.

Social workers said that the assessments that had been completed had been fully useful in only six of the 14 assessed cases (all but one on children aged two years or under). The assessments that social workers thought had been only partially useful were reported to be incomplete or to have addressed only some of the relevant issues. For example, the assessment of one child in a residential unit had not addressed important child protection issues relevant to her return home. Similarly, the assessment of an adolescent boy in a specialised unit had not included an assessment of his risk of re-offending. In another case the assessment of a mother had been incomplete because her circumstances kept changing.

The social workers' views on conditions for return

Only three of the social workers whom we interviewed spoke of conditions. In one case the conditions had been set out in a written agreement and approved by the court in care proceedings. These conditions were enforced and complied with and the social worker said that they had been useful in achieving clarity about expectations and assessing the mother's parenting ability to care for her small baby, and her commitment to change.

In another case, the conditions were set out in a written agreement attached to the care plan and required the mother to have treatment to address her mental health problems and drug and alcohol use. However, the social worker said that the conditions were not complied with and although this had not prevented the child's return home, these unresolved problems subsequently resulted in return breakdown. In the third case, the conditions set for the mother provided a very useful reminder of the expectations that professionals had of her if the return was to continue. However, there was no condition for *treatment* for this mother's drugs misuse and her life as a result was too chaotic for her to make use of the other services provided, so the return broke down.

In several cases the social workers who were interviewed had not been involved at the time of the return but expressed surprise that there was no evidence of a written agreement on file.

The social workers' views on professional support in preparation for the return

Twelve practitioners talked about work they had undertaken with parents prior to the child's return, which had focused on a range of issues including parenting skills and the management of the child's behaviour. Six of the social workers considered this work had been helpful. However, in the other six cases, little progress had been made because the parents had not co-operated or had not acknowledged their part in the children's problems. Other professionals had also undertaken work with parents in nine cases and the social workers considered this to have been very helpful in four. Direct work had been undertaken by the social worker with two of the children prior to the return home.

In a number of cases, social workers said that the children and/or their parents would have benefited from further work prior to the return home including, for example, a written agreement to establish clear expectations of everyone involved, work on a parent's alcohol or drug issues, and specialist therapeutic intervention for a physically abused child.

Overall, the interviews showed that interventions varied in how helpful they had been and that establishing a pattern of work required careful negotiations between social workers and parents, if co-operation was to be established. However, in a number of cases, assessments and interventions had not been provided (particularly for adolescents) and this was sometimes seen by social workers as having been because of a lack of co-operation from parents. The parents, in turn, had sometimes reported being distressed by the lack of help provided.

Now that assessment, conditions and work with children and families prior to return have been considered, in the next chapter we examine the children's pathways home.

Summary

- Younger children tended to have initial plans of time-limited assessment whereas return home was less likely to be in question for older children, unless there were significant concerns about abuse. These older children had often already experienced a number of failed returns home.

- The older children, who absconded or were returned home rapidly before a care plan had been formulated, had already typically oscillated in and out of care. It is important to note that this particularly problematic group of children received the least oversight whilst looked after.

- The children's initial care plans were key, as they were significantly related to whether the case was assessed or not and how quickly the children returned home.

- Altogether, fuller assessments (i.e. core or other agency assessments) were conducted for 57 per cent of the children and initial assessments alone for a further 8 per cent. Many of these assessments were multi-agency (43%) and where multi-agency assessments were conducted, children were more likely to be returned home safely.

- Assessment also led to better service provision. After assessment, two-thirds of parents and over half of the children received specialist support from children's services or another agency prior to the return, compared with only a third of parents and children whose circumstances had not been assessed.

- Where no work was undertaken with any family member (in 23% of cases), problems tended to persist into the return.

- The presence of conditions was linked to higher levels of service provision and seemed to assist in encouraging change.

- There had rarely been a condition imposed for obtaining treatment for drugs or alcohol misuse prior to return (and this was also true later during reunification) so this key opportunity to effect change had not been used.

Parent and social worker perspectives on planning for the children's returns

- The parents had been well aware that their parenting abilities were under scrutiny when they had small children but assessments of their behaviourally challenging adolescents were often lacking.
- Fifty-nine per cent of the parents interviewed considered that their social worker had worked actively towards the children returning to them and they were appreciative of this help. A number of parents said that they had wanted help for and with their children but that workers had not known how to deal with their children's behavioural and emotional difficulties.
- Some parents had found review meetings daunting, felt that their views were not listened to at such meetings or even that they were being put down.
- Parents were generally positive about mentors and youth offending workers for their children whilst they were looked after and a few children had had intensive treatment.
- The social workers whom we interviewed considered fewer than half of the assessments to have been fully useful to them and those which had been less useful had been incomplete or had only addressed some of the relevant issues.
- The social workers explained that in half of the cases parents had not co-operated with the direct work which they had planned to provide prior to the children's return, and these parents were often resistant to acknowledging their problems. In a number of cases social workers considered that the parents or children would have benefited from further work prior to return.

6 The children's pathways home

In this chapter we examine how the children's returns came about, including the kinds of pressures that were brought to bear on children's services to return the children home and, on the other hand, the barriers that occasionally delayed reunion. The preparations that were made for the returns are considered, as are the concerns that social workers or other professionals sometimes had about reunification taking place.

Pressures for the return

We found that pressures to return the children home affected three-quarters of the cases and came from many different sources. In almost two-thirds of the families, the parents, children or both, or less frequently a relative, strenuously pushed for the return to happen (see Table 6.1).

If children were accommodated (59%), the parents could ultimately take matters into their own hands and remove them from their placements, but where the child was subject to a care or interim care order (41%), this pressure could take the form of repeated complaints or requests, difficult behaviour or absconding by the child, or contests in court.

In a quarter of cases, there were pressures from the children's placements for them to move, and this prompted renewed consideration of the viability of return home. Pressure of this nature could arise because the placement was in difficulty; the caregivers encountered personal difficulties (such as illness or bereavement); the child did not get on with the caregivers' other children or because the behaviour of the children or parents was difficult. In a small number of cases there was some evidence to suggest that the children were deliberately sabotaging their placements in order to engineer their return home.

In nearly a tenth of cases, either the children's guardian or an expert witness had recommended return or, conversely, there was considered to be insufficient evidence for children's services to instigate care proceedings and thus no way the return home could be prevented, despite children's services staff fearing that it would be detrimental for the child.

In a small number of cases, children's services management or other agencies pressed for return, usually because of financial or policy pressures.

Often there was only one source of pressure for the return, but in a third of cases (32%) there were multiple pressures. In all, only just over a quarter of the children's social workers (26%) were able to consider what was in the child's best interests free from any pressures (see also Thoburn, 1980; Farmer and Parker, 1991). Pressures from parents were more likely to be exerted when the children were on interim or care orders rather than accommodated (57% compared with 37%), particularly when the return was being considered in the context of care proceedings.

Table 6.1
Pressures for the returns

	Total (n = 180)
No pressures	**26%**
Family pressures	**64%**
Pressure from either parent or child (aged 2+) (n = 147)	44%
Pressure from both	17%
Pressure from relatives	3%
Placement pressures	**25%**
Pressure because of child or parent behaviours	10%
Pressure because of carer circumstances (e.g. illness)	6%
Pressure because of placement shortages or instability	4%
Other placement pressures (e.g. carer thinks child should go home)	5%
Legal or management pressures	**11%**
Pressure because insufficient evidence to withstand legal challenge	1%
Pressure because children's guardian or expert opinion main driver for return	7%
Pressure from children's services management (e.g. budgetary)	2%
Pressure from other agency	1%

Barriers to return

It was encouraging to find that barriers to return were less frequent. The biggest barrier was lack of housing or inadequate accommodation, which affected 12 per cent of the families, followed by the social worker not completing the necessary work or paperwork (3%) and, finally, in a very small number of cases, lack of a school or day care place.

The children's evolving care plans

Perhaps then it is not surprising that for the majority of the children (61%), the decision to return them home had been made (and recorded on their care plans) within six months of them being looked after (for 28% on their first care plan). The remainder waited a year or more before the return decision was made or they returned home despite a plan *for return* never having been recorded on their file at any time.

The time that it took for the return decision to be made varied significantly with the legal status of the children and their initial care plans. Where children were accommodated, an early return home had been anticipated from the start and recorded on the first care plan for 39 per cent as compared with only 12 per cent of those on orders.

Where time-limited assessment was the initial plan, the decision to return the children home had usually been made within six months (58%), although for a quarter of these children, return plans were not made for a year or more. On the other hand, for a few children (16%), a plan for return was never recorded on their files.

For the children whose initial care plans were adoption or long-term care, it was the opposite story. The plans for very few of these children changed to return home within the first six months (7%) or a year (21%), with the majority of the decisions to return them (51%) being made between one and three years after the child started to be looked after. Researcher ratings suggested that it would not have been appropriate to make return plans any earlier for any of these children.

Most of the return decisions were made, or at least officially recorded as having been made, at statutory reviews (34%) or other children's services planning meetings (26%). An eighth (12%) were made as a result of court hearings or child protection reviews and a small number (12%) were made more informally with the parents, either face-to-face or over the telephone, usually in response to specific situations, for example, the child refusing to return to foster care after a home visit.

Parents had been present at most (87%) of the meetings where decisions were made by children's services, such as at child protection conferences, statutory reviews or other planning meetings. Foster carers or residential workers (caregivers) had attended for just over half of the time (54%) and children a quarter (25%).

Family and caregiver reservations about the return

Thus, most families and half of the caregivers had an opportunity to express their views and a small number (10% of parents, 8% of caregivers and 6% of children) were recorded as having expressed reservations about the return. Parents tended to have reservations about the returns because they were fearful about their own mental health or ability to cope or they were worried about what the child's behaviour would be like, particularly where children had been aggressive to their parents or beyond parental control. Children were concerned about being rejected or abused by their parents, about inconsistent parenting or being treated differently from their siblings. Caregivers could be afraid that the child was not ready to return home or that the home environment was not suitable. Cameron's story gives an example of parental concerns.

Cameron's story
When Cameron was ten, his mother, Liz, contacted children's services because he was self-harming, head-banging, soiling and shoplifting. Liz was depressed and had recently attempted suicide. Following an incident where Cameron was violent and abusive to his mother, he was accommodated. The initial care plan was for Cameron to return home within three months if his relationship with Liz improved. Liz, however, was reluctant to have Cameron home for overnight stays and would not commit to a date for his

---

return. She said that she could not bear to be around him and would not be able to look after him as she had found a part-time job. Despite his mother's concerns, he was returned home with a package of support. A year later this return broke down after Cameron, who was depressed and truanting from school, was thrown out of the home by Liz.

Professional concerns about the returns

Professionals, on the other hand, expressed concerns about just over a third of the returns. Social workers expressed reservations about a quarter of them as did 16 per cent of the other professionals, such as psychologists or guardians.

Professional concerns tended to emphasise the risks that remained for the child (67%), the effects the return might have on the child's behaviour (24%) or how the return could affect a parent or sibling (9%). Professionals significantly often expressed concerns where children were returning to an emotionally abusive parent or to a family where they had previously experienced multiple adversities.

Where the court was actively involved with the case, in two cases the court ordered a return against the wishes of the local authority and in three others the court ruled against reunification when children's services had considered that return was in the child's best interests.

Factors influencing the return decisions

Where return decisions were made and recorded on the child's care plan, we noted what had made reunification possible, with up to three issues recorded in each case. A crucial facilitator influencing the decision was improved professional support (35%), with greater safety for the child (25%), improvements in the parents' relationship with the child (25%) or in the parents' parenting skills (24%) also important (see also Wade et al, 2011). Other key factors influencing the decision were increased parental motivation, better housing conditions, improvements in the child's

Table 6.2
Factors facilitating the returns

	Primary facilitator (n = 151)	Secondary facilitator (n = 151)	Tertiary facilitator (n = 151)	Total (n = 151)
Improved professional support	14%	8%	13%	**35%**
Improved safety for the child	18%	6%	1%	**25%**
Improved relationship with the child	6%	11%	8%	**25%**
Improved parenting skills	10%	6%	8%	**24%**
Improved motivation to parent the child	6%	8%	6%	**20%**
Improved housing or home conditions	3%	11%	1%	**15%**
Improved child's behaviour	7%	2%	3%	**12%**
Improved parental mental health	7%	4%	1%	**12%**
Improved parental stability or maturity	2%	7%	3%	**12%**
Improved substance misuse	6%	2%	2%	**10%**
Improved social support	3%	6%	–	**9%**
Parent discharged from hospital	2%	3%	–	**5%**
Essential service provided	1%	1%	2%	**4%**
Reduced domestic violence	1%	1%	1%	**3%**
Improved couple relating	1%	–	1%	**2%**
Improved parent employment	1%	1%	–	**2%**
Parent released from prison	1%	–	1%	**2%**
None	11%	23%	49%	
Total	100%	100%	100%	100%

behaviour, parental mental health or parental stability (see Table 6.2). In 11 per cent of cases there was no evidence that any specific changes had influenced the return decision.

However, what was striking from the case file reviews was how often other issues that had the potential to jeopardise the success of the returns remained unresolved or hidden from children's services. These were most frequently undisclosed or underestimated drug or alcohol problems or continuing relationships with abusive partners. Shelley's story gives an example of such a scenario.

Shelley's story

Shelley was accommodated following concerns about her mother's neglect and rejection of her and Shelley's behavioural problems. Work concentrated on the mother–daughter relationship but concerns about the mother's debt and drug use were not dealt with. Shelley returned home after there was a dramatic improvement in her behaviour. A month later the mother was arrested for possession of drugs and stolen goods. Shelley was again accommodated and care proceedings were initiated.

Planning and pressures for return

In Chapter 5 we saw that the initial plans for 41 per cent of the children had been for reunification. By the time of the return, this was the plan for three-quarters (73%) of them. However, as can be seen in Figure 6.1, over a quarter (27%) of the children returned home in the absence of a plan for return *at that time*, including six per cent who returned home before there had been time for any care plan to be formulated, and the remaining 21 per cent had plans in place for time-limited assessment, shared care or permanence plans (including for adoption) at the time of their returns.

Where a plan for return was in force at the time of the return (73%, 131), a clear account of the reasoning for the return occurring at that time was recorded on file in only two-thirds of the cases (65%). For the remainder it was not clear from the file why the decision to return the

Figure 6.1
The children's care plans at the time of their return

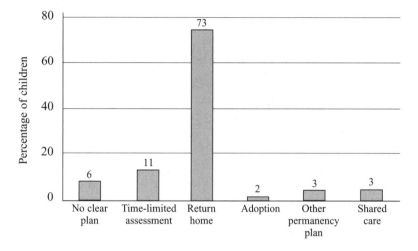

child had been taken (see also Farmer and Parker, 1991).

Where the reasons for the return decision were recorded, improve-ments in the family situation or the child's behaviour were only noted as having been the primary reason for the return in just under half (48%) of the cases (see Table 6.3). In these situations the parents had been judged to be safer or better able to cope, or there had been a favourable change in the family composition – usually an abusive parent leaving but occasion-ally a supportive partner moving in – or more rarely, the child had demon-strated a marked change in his or her behaviour since being looked after.

Other main reasons for the returns included that return had always been the plan, that is, that only a temporary period of care had ever been envisaged (22%) or the court had ordered reunification (2%). In 16 per cent of cases the parent or child had pressed for the return, or decided that it was time for reunion in situations where the child had been accommodated, whilst in 10 per cent the child's placement was facing breakdown or was due to end. Indeed, in a third of cases, the return was accelerated because of such reasons, that is, it happened earlier than had originally been planned, whilst in nearly one in five cases the children

Table 6.3
Reasons given for the planned returns (n = 131)

	Primary reason (n = 131)	Secondary reason (n = 131)	Total (n = 131)
Improvements within the family	48%	37%	85%
Parent better able to cope/safer	31%	19%	50%
Favourable change in family composition	12%	2%	14%
Parent comes out of prison/hospital	2%	2%	4%
Child's good behaviour	3%	6%	9%
Housing/material circumstances improved	–	8%	8%
Official decision	24%	15%	39%
Return always the plan (SSD decision)	22%	8%	30%
Court ordered return	2%	7%	9%
Parent or child pressure or request	16%	16%	32%
Parent request or pressure	9%	14%	23%
Child distress or request	5%	1%	6%
Child's absconding	2%	1%	3%
Placement breakdown or ending	10%	9%	19%
Placement threatened or actual breakdown	5%	2%	7%
Placement inappropriate or ending	3%	5%	8%
No suitable alternative placement available	1%	1%	1%
Care not working out	1%	1%	1%
None	–	19%	19%
Other	2%	4%	6%
Total	**100%**	**100%**	

were returned home for further assessment of the viability of their family situation.

Table 6.3 illustrates both the primary and secondary reasons for the planned returns. It is important to underline that, whilst improvements in the family accounted for almost half (48%) of the primary reasons for return, pressures from the parent, child (16%), placement (10%) or the court (2%) accounted for another quarter (28%).

As we have seen, more than a quarter of the children returned home in the absence of a plan to do so and there were a variety of situations in which this occurred. Sometimes, children had returned home because they had absconded there or remained at home after a contact visit (27%), others had been removed from voluntary accommodation by their parents (15%), or their placement had broken down (11%) or was ending and no suitable alternative placement was available (8%). At other times, parents had come out of hospital or prison earlier than planned (10%) or, in almost a third of these cases (29%), the social worker had agreed to a return home (despite there being no official plan for return) because there had been improvements, however short term, in the family situation.

Preparation for the returns

Where the returns were planned, specific preparations for the children's returns were made for a third (36%) of them. Usually (19%) this was work with the parents on the impact that the child's return would have on the family or discussion of the behavioural problems they might experience, but in a small number of cases (6%), work was conducted with the children to prepare them for going home or, more often, with both the parent and child together (11%). Only a third of the children over the age of four (36%) were consulted about the timing or manner in which they were to return home (although such conversations might not have been recorded on file).

When planned, many (62%) of the returns were intended to be gradual and to include increasing day visits or overnight stays prior to the child's full-time return home. The majority (49%) of these "phased returns" worked out as planned, but in a small number (13%) the child or parent decided that the child would stay at home before the agreed return date. This was usually because the parents did not understand the merits of a gradual return home or because the child was distressed at the thought of having to return to care again, albeit briefly.

Social work support to the families at this vulnerable time was variable, but face-to-face visits were not very frequent, with just a fifth of parents and children (20% and 19% respectively) seeing their social worker every fortnight or more, on average, in the three months prior to the return. Over half (56% and 57% respectively) had only seen the social worker once a month or less often and (of these) just over a quarter (26% and 28%) only once or not at all in this three-month period. Occasionally, children went to live with the other parent (that is, not the parent they were removed from) in the absence of any visits or assessment from children's services, despite previous worrying incidents of that parent's behaviour having been recorded on file.

Nonetheless, many returns (57%) were supported with a package of services that had been agreed prior to, or at the same time as, the return. These support packages could include regular respite care, ongoing support or intervention from mental health services or other agencies or, in some cases, financial or material support. (This is explored further in the next chapter.) Researcher ratings indicated that, taking these packages into consideration, just over half of the families (52%) had been adequately resourced and supported prior to the returns such that they had a reasonable chance of success. In the remainder of cases, it was considered that families would have benefited from additional support in relation to child management, mental health problems, substance misuse or from additional or more thorough assessment of their circumstances.

Returning home

When it came to the actual return home, the children's caregivers could be vital to the smoothness or otherwise of the transition, either encouraging and supporting the child and family in their attempts to make the return work or being the source of problems. Caregivers could find relinquishing children difficult if they were very strongly attached to them or did not consider return home to be in their best interests (see also Farmer and Dance *et al*, 2010), or disputes could arise over retained clothing or possessions. Some caregivers, however, gave exceptional support prior to the returns (19%) and often continued to befriend and support the family after the return. The support at this stage of some social workers (12%) was also considered to be exceptional.

Legal status at the time of the returns

During the time the children were looked after, little changed overall in terms of their legal status. Three-fifths of the children were accommodated at the time of their returns (59%) and the remainder were subject to interim care orders (24%) or care orders (13%) and the returns were therefore made under The Placements with Parents etc Regulations 1991. Four per cent of the children returned on supervision orders.

The parents' views of precipitants for return

When we reviewed the circumstances that had finally facilitated the study returns to the 34 parents whom we interviewed, we found that in just four cases some kind of improvement in the parents led to the return. In one, this concerned a cessation of drinking; in two, improvements in the mother's mental state; and, in one other, the parents of a boy in a residential unit had attended a parenting course to assist them in dealing with their son. In eight other cases, children returned after some kind of assessment had been completed, and in two of these, this was also assisted by the provision of suitable accommodation so that mothers could take their babies into the community from a mother and baby foster placement.

In four other cases, a change in household composition (for example, a child who had been living with both parents returned to the mother or father alone or moved to the other parent) had made return possible. (In two of these, lone parents were also ably supported by their own parents.) Four other children returned home because of a change in parental circumstances, such as re-marriage, a move to a larger house or a parent leaving prison. Thus, in 20 cases, the parental situation had changed in some way, however small, or an assessment had concluded that the parents could care for the children.

In just two cases, improvements in the children's behaviour was considered to have led to the return, and a third child had returned to his parents because he wanted to be at home after 14 months in care.

As we will see, in another 10 cases, children went home either because their placement broke down, the parents removed them from the placement, or the child absconded home.

The parents' views on the decision for the children to return to them

In 10 of the 34 parent interview cases (29%), there was little or no opportunity for formal decision-making for reunification since the parents, child or placement precipitated the return. In five of these cases, the children returned home because the parent had removed them from their placements, in two cases because of sexual abuse or involvement in sexualised behaviour. In four other cases, placement breakdown led directly to return, on two occasions because the study child or another foster child had made an allegation against the foster carers.

In the interviews we asked the parents who had decided that the children would return to them. Of the 34 parents, 14 (41%) said that the social worker had determined that the child would return, six (18%) saw it as a joint decision by the social workers and themselves, 10 (29%) as determined by them and the remainder were placement disruptions. It is worth noting that, whilst parents saw a significant group of decisions as having been taken by social workers alone, the social workers considered all their decisions to have been made jointly with parents.

Decisions made by the social workers

Of the parents who said that the social worker had decided on the return, several described meetings at which the decision was taken – some of which were statutory reviews or child protection review meetings – with a few commenting that they had had no influence on the decision but others feeling that everyone was involved or at least that they had agreed with the decision.

In most of the cases where mothers were in mother and baby placements or residential assessment units, it was clear that the decision for the mother (or parents) and baby to live in the community (which was regarded as the return) was made by the social worker and other agencies involved, after they had assessed the parents' capacity to care. Sometimes, as we have seen, assessments had also involved other professionals such as a psychologist. Some parents knew that they had had to prove that they could cope with their children and were well enough and capable of doing so. For example, in one case, after serious injuries to a baby caused by the father, the mother felt that the subsequent assessments had been long drawn out and had lasted a long time before the decision was made for the children to be returned to her. She said:

> *I did all the assessments. I did all the work with them, healthy eating and all this palaver . . . going with them to x and y . . . to the foster carers' home to see them and everything.*

One mother was concerned that her daughter, Robyn, was feeling left out of the family whilst in care but she also knew that her presence in the family had a negative impact on her other children. She had found this a difficult situation and said:

> *I didn't feel I got very much support with that kind of decision really. They said 'If you can't cope she won't go home'. I needed them to offer a perspective on this situation.*

At the same time she knew:

> *It was a case of you know 'We'll decide' . . . they were calling the shots . . . I needed reassurance . . . They don't care what the mother thinks. They only focus on the child . . . I had to constantly do things exactly how they want. I felt I couldn't say what I wanted.*

Eventually, children's services did suggest that Robyn return and the mother agreed. However, she had not really sorted out how to manage her other children; they were ambivalent about their sister returning; the mother's discipline was inconsistent and she was very anxious about how she would cope. She said:

> *It was a very mixed feeling about her coming back home.*

The return of 12-year-old Julie, which was decided at review, was seen by the girl herself as a decision over which she had some influence. She said:

> *I demanded and my mum thought it was a good idea and my social worker decided it was a good idea . . . because I didn't get on with the*

foster carers who accused me of things . . . The social worker was very nice and thought I was mature enough to go home . . . [The decision] was made at a meeting . . . I could say what I wanted.

Seven-year-old Tracey who was returned, on the social worker's decision, to her mother, who had an alcohol problem and had neglected her, said that she had returned home because she was better behaved. However, she added that she had not told anyone about her other feelings:

I did want to stay there [in care], come back and see Mum but go back again, because I felt there was more space for Mum and more space for me. I did enjoy it more [in care] than staying here, so I wouldn't have hassle from Mum and I wouldn't give hassle to her.

Of these 14 cases, where the social workers had made the decision to return, all but one child was under the age of 10 at return. Thus, it appears easier for social workers to take the decision and determine when return will occur for younger children. Returns were often less straightforward for the older children.

Decisions that were jointly made by parents and social workers

When parents reported that the decision was a joint one between them and the social workers, all six children had been over the age of 10 at return. In one case, the mother said that the social worker had told her that her son of 13 had improved a lot and he could return when the mother felt it was right. He did return, although his mother did not feel quite ready and her new partner did not want her son at home. Her son's view of the situation was similar to his mother's:

The social worker decided I could go home because I was being good. The social worker asked me once if I wanted to go home.

Similarly, another mother saw the decision as a joint one with children's services in which she chose the date. However, her 13-year-old daughter had a rather different experience:

*I was in care temporarily to let things cool down and to have a break.
I don't know how it was decided [about return]. I remember packing.
That was it . . .*

However, some joint decisions were for less positive reasons. For
example, one boy of 12 returned to his mother after 14 months of being
looked after because, according to his mother, children's services 'could
not do anything with him' and she agreed to have him home, although she
and her husband did not feel prepared. She thought that on hearing that
the parents were prepared to have their son back, the department:

. . . must have had a party . . . put the flags out the window.

Decisions made by the parents

In 10 cases, the parents had seen themselves as the prime movers in the
return. Seven of these children were over the age of 10 at return. It was
interesting to find that when parents precipitated returns, they had nonetheless often not felt ready for the children. For example, the mother who
took her 10-year-old daughter home after only two days in a foster
placement said that her daughter had been crying and was in danger and
had begged her on the telephone to take her home. However, she said that
neither she nor her daughter had really been ready to live together. Her
daughter, Mandy, said that she had wanted to go to another foster
placement and was worried about going home to her unpredictable
mother, who had mental health problems.

Only two of these returns that were decided by the parents took place
for positive reasons. One mother said that she and the stepfather decided
to have her 14-year-old daughter home because 'she had changed so
much' after two years of being looked after and was behaving better. The
other positive return involved a father who had taken on the care of his
disabled son as soon as he had managed to sell his business and buy a
house for them.

Return because of placement breakdown

The four children who returned home because of placement breakdowns
all went on to have failed returns. In one case, a children's home refused

to have a 10-year-old girl back after three months because of her difficult behaviour. The mother said:

She didn't have a choice. We didn't have a choice.

Another mother considered that the situation when her daughter came home was '100 per cent worse' than before, because of her daughter's rejection by the foster carer:

And she just dumped her. Literally, no clothes, nothing. Not a single item of her things came back. And that's the way it ended up.

Thus, in all, in the parent interview sample two in five children (14 of the 34) returned for reasons outside the social workers' control, either because of sudden placement disruption or because the parents decided on the return or pulled their children out of their placements, generally because of well-founded concerns about the safety or progress of the placement. This echoes the findings of earlier research on reunification, which found that in only a minority of cases did children return as a result of planned reunification and return often occurred at the instigation of the parents (Thoburn, 1980; Farmer and Parker, 1991). In only another two in five cases (14) had the social worker been the main player in deciding the return, and this was principally in relation to younger children. In the remainder, reunification was worked out between the parents and social worker.

As we have seen, in a few cases, the parents' ability to care for their children was carefully assessed, for example, for those in mother and baby placements or when a small child had suffered injuries. In two cases, children were returned to their parents on the recommendation of the children's guardian and a psychiatrist in direct opposition to local authority plans for adoption. In other cases, reunification depended more on a perception that children were not gaining from being looked after, or a placement had ended or broken down or a worse placement was being avoided, whether or not the children or parents had made changes. In fact, it was rare for the parents to say that either they or the child had made improvements. Occasionally, return occurred because of a change in parental circumstances that made it possible for them to resume care.

What is striking is how often the parents themselves harboured doubts about the wisdom of return at that time and about their own ability to cope or said that they did not feel prepared or felt ambivalent, even when they had instigated the return. Interestingly, doubts were expressed not only when reunification occurred because of placement breakdown but also when the decision had been taken by the social worker and parents together and by parents alone.

It is also worth noting that a few children would have preferred to remain looked after, although they had not always been able to make this known. The children's accounts of how the decision was made for them to return home varied and were often somewhat different from those of their parents, as we will see later in this chapter. But first, we consider the parents' views on preparation and support for the returns.

The parents' views on preparation and support for the returns

Of the 24 parent interviews where preparation could have been made, three-fifths of the parents mentioned some preparation (14). Such preparation, broadly interpreted, took a number of forms. In some cases, it was extensive. For example, one mother, who had an alcohol misuse problem, had a social worker who had 'stuck with her' through numerous false starts at treatment, as well as supportive parents who had often looked after the children when she could not. Whilst Julie and her brother were looked after, the mother had attended Alcoholics Anonymous (AA) and had been well supported by her social worker. As she said:

I've always had social services nagging me – they've been marvellous . . . If I had a drink he [the social worker] knows about it.

She had also had help from a family support worker who 'came whenever I wanted her' and with whom the mother could talk. In contrast, her daughter, Julie, did not report being prepared for the return, although she had been visiting her mother for weekends for some time previously.

Another mother had visited her baby frequently while he was in foster care and had helped to bathe him, so ensuring that she maintained her relationship with her son and became accustomed to caring for him.

Similarly, the social worker had carefully prepared the parents of a four-month-old baby for his return and talked to them about how he might be unsettled at night and how to handle him and the mother had attended a mother and baby group for support. (She had also had extensive support from her parents.) Staff from a residential unit, in another case, had met regularly with the boy's mother to explain their work, provide input and discuss how she could help to integrate her son into the family on his return.

Parents who left residential assessment centres or mother and baby foster placements sometimes mentioned getting help with housing, nursery places, referrals for counselling or financial help.

A number of mothers described careful preparation for the children to return although they were negative about the social workers' part in this. This might partly reflect the social workers' power to delay or withhold return. For example, one mother who was depressed and disabled received help from a family support worker at what she saw as 'an overwhelming time in my life'. However, she found it hard to accept the support provided because:

I felt they were getting at me a lot as well.

She had help from her GP who put her on new anti-depressants and she saw a counsellor at one stage. She felt that the newly qualified social worker allocated to her case was 'emotionally detached', belittled her and had no respect. This social worker helped with transport and stipulated that this mother attend a family centre. On the other hand, the mother was very positive about the foster carers, whom she saw as:

. . . very helpful . . . She helped me look at things and decide better than social workers.

Her daughter, Amina, herself had a support worker in school for her behaviour, which had been very helpful.

In other cases, preparation was more limited. For example, some parents recalled only that the children's social worker had visited once or twice prior to their children's return to discuss it.

Whilst these examples of preparation range from the extensive to the cursory, other parents had not received any preparation for their children's return. This was especially likely to occur with the older children.

The children's views of the decision for return

We asked the children whose idea it was that they should return home. Their views revealed a somewhat different perspective from that of their parents. Four did not know, five said the idea came from their parents, six from the social worker, two from the child and two jointly from parents, the child and social worker.

One girl, who had returned home at the age of seven, said that the decision had been made by the social worker:

The boss at social services decided I could return because Mum was doing well. She wasn't drinking, except on special occasions. She wouldn't go out all the time and get drunk.

Another girl who had returned at the age of nine said:

It was the social worker's idea that I should return home . . . They worried how much it was costing and I was behaving better and not running away . . . I didn't know how long it was planned I'd be in care – they didn't talk to me very long . . . I wanted to come home . . . [although] I was a bit worried I'd kick off again and have to leave home.

A girl who had returned at the age of 10 said:

I think social services and that thought it would be alright if I went back and that my mum would be able to cope.

She thought that her mother, who had mental health problems, was a lot better and wanted her back. The decision had been made at a review at which the child had been able to say a little about what she had wanted.

One 11-year-old boy thought that the social worker and foster carers had decided together when he could return but recognised his mother's reluctance to have him back:

I'd changed, not as stressed, more grown-up because Mum didn't let me grow up ... Mum didn't want me back but had to take me eventually. I wanted to return.

A girl who felt that she had been influential in the decision said:

I told my social worker before the [review] meeting. I said that I was going home, whether he liked it or not. So I came home.

In contrast, one boy, who recalled not having had the courage to say what he thought about returning, said that it had been either the social worker's or his mother's idea for him to return:

To see how it would turn out. See if I could stay there instead of going into care ... It was just like the social worker was trying to control my life. I wanted to go back home and forget it all.

Some children described events that had precipitated the return, such as assaulting a child in the placement or getting into a fight with another child, even on one occasion making it clear that they had engineered the return in this way. On the other hand, a small number of children expressed worries or serious reservations about returning at all to their parents or felt that the timing was wrong and two would rather have remained in their placements.

There was little to suggest that the children had been extensively consulted about the returns, except in a minority of cases, and a few felt angry that they had not been able to return earlier. In all, of those interviewed, seven of the young people thought that they had been able to express their views fully about returning home and another four had done so partially, although eight had not. Whilst most of the 19 children were happy at the prospect of returning home, five were worried about it or scared.

The children's views on preparation and support for their returns

Before returning to their parents, nine of the young people had felt fully prepared for the return and five partially prepared, but five had not felt prepared at all.

The children had clear views about the need for preparation for return. In some cases, the parents had been prepared but not the children, whilst in others, young people said that their social worker had talked to them about returning, even when the parents had not been prepared in this way.

For example, a girl who had returned home at the age of nine had discussed this with her social worker and was having weekly counselling sessions. She had felt fully prepared. One boy, who went home at the age of 12, had had regular visits from his social worker but he commented that a trial week might have been useful.

A girl, who had not been prepared (although her mother had been), said:

I got my stuff and went home.

Another girl, who had not felt prepared, recalled:

Packing my bags and being taken back.

Ten-year-old Mandy, who returned when her mentally ill mother removed her from foster care, said that she had needed some visits home first and considered that she had gone home too quickly. Fourteen-year-old Sheila said she too had needed more notice of the return. She wished that she had had 'the opportunity to talk to people to decide if it was the best thing for me', so that she could have decided against return if she had wished to, since she had not wanted to go home. Seven-year-old Tracey, who was returned to her mother, who misused alcohol, said that she had not told anyone that she had wanted to stay in care and not go home.

Although most of the help to prepare children came from social workers, three young people had talked to their foster mothers and received advice from them about going home in relation to such things as their behaviour, schooling and how to deal with a parent's new partner.

The social workers' views on the decisions to return and changes in plans for the children

In the interviews, the social workers spoke of a small number of cases where the local authority had not been in agreement with the return (which had been instigated by the parents) but that they had not been in a position to oppose it, and also of cases where children's services had agreed with a return which they had not initiated, although the social workers had been unhappy about it. In one of these, the child returned to the parent only because there was no suitable alternative care placement.

The social workers' perspectives on the appropriateness of the children's returns

Ten out of the 14 social workers who talked about how appropriate reunification had been had had concerns as to whether the return had been in the child's best interests and as to whether it would work out in the long term. In a few of these cases, the return had been brought forward under pressure from the parents or parents had removed children from placements. In addition, half of the children or parents had problems which, in the view of the social workers, had not been addressed prior to the children's return home. (The proportion in the case file sample was 22%.) None of these returns was successful. The reasons given by social workers for the problems not having been addressed all related to difficulties in engaging the family in work, rather than with the availability of services, for example, a mother's unwillingness to accept help with her drug problem or another mother's intractable mental health problems.

The social workers' views on contingency planning

The interviews revealed that there was considerable variability in the quality of planning for children if the return home did not work out successfully.

In five cases, social workers said that specific contingency plans had been put in place in case the returns did not work out and these had been discussed and were clearly understood by the child and family. These included, for example, a plan for children to return to the foster carer with whom they had previously been placed and who was kept on a retainer to provide support to the family for six months following the return and placement for a boy with the foster carer who was providing him with respite care twice a week.

For other children, contingency planning was more general such as that, in the event of breakdown, children would return to care or long-term alternative care plans would be made.

The social workers' views on support services in preparation for the returns

In 10 cases, social workers said that support services were planned and in place prior to the children's return home. For some families the planned packages of services were comprehensive and complex and in addition to social work input included, in individual cases, for example: CAMHS worker and school support; respite care, educational assistance and clinical psychologist support; sessions at a Child and Adolescent Family Therapy Service; psychotherapy for the parents, financial advice and support; daily contact from a family support worker, health visitor and 24 hour "on call" support from the foster carer; family support worker, a nursery place, individual psychotherapy for the mother, home care worker, respite care and foster carer support.

However, in four cases no support services were planned, in one case because of the parents' unwillingness to work with their social worker, even though the child was subject to a care order.

Now that we have examined the children's pathways home, we look in the next chapter at the children's experiences when they returned to their parents.

Summary

- Where time-limited assessment was the initial plan, the decision for children to return home was usually made within six months (58%), whereas when adoption or long-term care were the initial plan, the majority of the return decisions (82%) were not made for between one and three years.
- Pressures to return the children home came from the parents, children or wider family members (64%), from placements disrupting or

experiencing other difficulties (25%) or from legal or management sources (12%). Only just over a quarter of returns (26%) were free from any pressures.

- Professional concerns were raised about the returns in just over a third of cases, particularly where a child was being returned to an emotionally abusive parent or to a family where he or she had experienced multiple adversities. Reservations about the returns were recorded on the case files for only a small number of parents (10%), caregivers (9%) or children (6%), although the interviews revealed that a considerable number of parents and some children had reservations.

- The single most important factor influencing the decision for return was that the safety of the child had improved (18%). However, issues which might jeopardise reunification often remained unresolved or hidden from children's services.

- Where the reasons for the return decision were recorded, improvements in the family situation or the child's behaviour were only noted as having been the primary reasons for the returns in just under half of the cases (48%).

- A third of the children over the age of four were recorded on file as having been consulted about the timing or manner in which they were to return home. Specific preparations for the children's returns were recorded as made in only a third of cases.

Parents', children's and social workers' perceptions of the children's pathways home

- In some cases, the parents' ability to care for their children was carefully assessed or return occurred because of a beneficial change in parental circumstances, but in other cases, reunification depended more on a perception that children were not gaining from being looked after or a placement had broken down. It was rare for the parents to say that either they or the child had made improvements. It was striking how often the parents themselves harboured doubts about the wisdom of return at that time and about their own ability to cope or said that they did not feel prepared, even when they had instigated the return.

- The children's accounts of how the decision for them to return to a parent was made were often somewhat different from those of their parents. There was little to suggest that the children had been extensively consulted about the returns, except in a minority of cases, and two had not wanted to return at all.

- Ten out of the 14 social workers who talked about this issue had had concerns as to whether the return had been in the child's best interests or would work out in the long term. The reasons given by social workers for the parents' problems not having been addressed all related to difficulties in engaging the family in work.
- Specific contingency plans if the return home did not work out successfully had been made for five of the 14 children for whom we had this information from social workers.

7 The children go home

This chapter focuses on the experiences of the children when they went home. We describe how their family situations had changed since they had gone into care and review the characteristics and behaviours of their parents. The monitoring and support provided for the returns are considered, as are the practices associated with returning children home subject to care or supervision orders or to child protection procedures. The progress of the returns is described in the next chapter.

The children's families at return

Whilst almost two-thirds of the children (64%) returned to the same parents (or parent figures) with whom they had lived previously, a quarter (26%) returned to families where a parent or partner (or other relative) had left or joined the household since they had been in care, and a tenth returned to a different family unit altogether (see Table 7.1).

Children who returned to exactly the same parents and parent figures

Table 7.1
Changes in family composition

	Total *(n = 180)*
No changes in carers	**64%**
Same family but change in carers	**26%**
Parent was with partner, now alone	11%
Parent was with partner, now with different partner	3%
Parent was alone, now with partner	10%
Kin left or joined the household	2%
Different family unit	**10%**
Was with one parent, now with other who is alone	4%
Was with one parent, now with other with their partner	4%
Was with kin, now with parent	2%

also tended to return to the same address (84%), whereas most children (60%) who experienced changes in their carers also needed to adjust to a different home.

These changes were frequently accompanied by changes in the children or other adults in the family (that is, lodgers, friends or siblings' partners) and, even where the carers did not change, new siblings could be born into the family or grown-up siblings leave, such that a quarter of the children experienced changes in the siblings who were at home (including 10% who had new baby siblings) and a few experienced changes in the other adults. In total, only just over half of the children (52%) did not experience *any* changes in the members of their household but, as a fifth of those went home to new addresses, only two-fifths (42%) went back to *exactly* the same home situation they had left.

When compared with the families from which they had been removed, children went to fewer two-parent families (9% as compared with 17% prior to care) and slightly more single parent and parent and partner families (58% compared with 55% and 29% compared with 26% respectively).

On their return, a few children (8%) went to live with a new female carer (mostly birth mothers or stepmothers) and rather more (18%) a new male carer (their birth father or a stepfather or mother's partner). Two-fifths of the children (43%) returned to homes where their siblings were already living (because they had remained at home or been returned home earlier), whilst a third were returned with one or more of their siblings. As a result, only a quarter of the children were the only child in the new household, whilst the remainder lived with one to four siblings. In addition, almost a tenth of the children also had siblings who remained in care.

During the course of the study return, some of these siblings later returned home, new siblings were born and parental partnerships changed, so that by the end of the two-year follow-up period (or the return ending if sooner) only a third of the children (36%) had not experienced any changes of household since the time they were looked after.

Previous abuse and neglect and parental difficulties

As well as adapting to changes in their household membership, physical location, school (26%) and day care arrangements, three-quarters of the children (76%) were returned to parents who had previously maltreated them or their siblings or were suspected of having done so, with the attendant anxiety this provoked. These were mostly mothers (52%) or stepmothers, more rarely fathers, stepfathers or mother's partners (8%) or both parents or a parent and their partner (16%). Over half of the time (55%) the abuse or neglect had been denied.

A small number of children (3%) were, unusually, returned to a parent who was thought to have sexually abused them. This occurred where there had been some uncertainty about the allegation, sometimes because the young people had retracted their allegations when it became clear that they could not otherwise return home. Notably, however, concerns about the safety of all of these children had been raised either before or after they went home.

Most children (82%) were also returned to parents who had a history of domestic violence, drug or alcohol misuse or exposure to inappropriate sexual activity (such as prostitution or open use of pornography), or several of these; all of which were likely to affect the parenting they received. As we saw in Chapter 3, mental health problems had also been diagnosed in relation to half (52%) of the mothers and a tenth (11%) of the fathers, whilst 10 per cent of the mothers and five per cent of the fathers had learning difficulties. A few children were returned to parents where either both had mental health problems or both had learning difficulties. Physical health problems or disabilities also affected just over a tenth of the families.

Over two-fifths of the carers (42%) also had a history of ambivalence when it came to parenting the child, for example, being indifferent about the return or seeming enthusiastic about it but acting in ways that were inconsistent with this, for example, not visiting when they could or not taking action that would have facilitated the return.

Whilst for almost two-thirds of the children (62%) this was the first time a return to these parents had been tried, more than a third of the children had already been unsuccessfully returned to these parents once (26%) or more often (12%).

The returns were only fully sanctioned in two-thirds (65%) of the cases (that is, a return plan was in place *and* the timing of the return had been agreed), with improvements in the family situation or the child's behaviour recorded as the primary reason for the return in just under half of these 117 cases (which equates to just under a third of the whole sample).

In only a quarter of cases (26%) were *all* the problems that had led to the child entering care considered by the researchers to have been adequately addressed, such that the return could be undertaken safely. The remainder of the children had returned home because of pressure from various sources, inadequacies in the care system or in order that there could be a continuing assessment of the parent's capacity to care for the child. In two-fifths of cases (42%), there had been no assessment of the family situation (or only an initial assessment) and in a quarter (24%), no services had been provided for the parents or child during the time that the child was looked after.

Monitoring of the return

There was therefore a need for good monitoring and support of the return in most cases. This was facilitated in almost half (47%) of them by the children being on supervision orders, interim or care orders (41%) or being the subject of child protection plans (28%). A fifth of the children (21%) were monitored by both systems.

Children who were neither on court orders nor a child protection plan (53%) were less well monitored (see below). However, for almost a fifth of the children, support and oversight were short-lived, with their cases being closed within six months of their return home, whilst for a tenth of families a social worker was never allocated to the case during the return or never visited the family home. Indeed, perhaps because of caseload pressures, by the end of the two-year follow-up period almost half the cases (48%) had been closed.

As would be expected, cases were less likely to be closed if children were under a care or supervision order (62% of these cases remained open throughout the duration of the follow-up period compared with 38% of cases of children who were not under orders).

Worryingly, almost half (47%) of these closed cases were closed despite ongoing concerns, including some that were substantial. Often, however, closing cases in these circumstances was short lived. In total, almost half (45%) of the closed cases had to be re-opened once or more before the end of the two-year follow-up period and this may have contributed to a lack of continuity of social work oversight, since in half of all the cases, the allocated social worker changed once (32%) or more (18%) during the follow-up period.

Social worker visits and case supervision

Whilst cases were open, a third of the social workers (35%) visited regularly at least every two months, with some visiting fortnightly (14%) and a few (8%) visiting weekly or more often. Two-fifths visited at very variable intervals (although not necessarily infrequently) and the remainder (25%) visited once every two to three months or less often (sometimes because of case closures or because the return failed very quickly).

Children were always or usually seen by social workers just under half of the time (46%) and occasionally or sometimes a third (32%) of the time. The remaining children – a fifth (22%) – were rarely or never seen by their social worker during the return. Whilst for half of these cases this was not surprising, since they were closed or broke down within six weeks, it is of some concern in the wake of baby Peter Connelly's case (Haringey Local Safeguarding Children Board (LSCB) 2008 and 2009) that the other half of the children were so rarely seen by their social worker, especially as a few them (9%) were subject to child protection plans or court orders.

However, one explanation for this may be the high level of supervision that was conducted by other agencies (61%), which occurred significantly more often where children were on court orders and somewhat more often for those subject to child protection plans. The weight and growth of a fifth of the children were monitored and a quarter (24%) were monitored for school or nursery attendance.

Children subject to child protection plans were also regularly monitored by means of their child protection reviews, whilst all the children on court orders were subject to looked after children reviews, although a fifth of these were conducted later than the statutory six-monthly intervals. Reviews were, on the whole, well attended by parents (90%) and children aged eight or over (59%). Most families were not difficult to contact but a fifth of the social workers had difficulty contacting the parent or child or getting them to engage. Interestingly, this was not related to whether the children were on orders or subject to child protection plans.

Conditions during the return

Conditions were imposed in almost two-fifths (39%) of cases as a means of facilitating positive change or engagement with services, particularly where children were subject to care or supervision orders (65%) or on child protection plans (73%). Indeed, they were rarely imposed where no order was in force (21%) or there had been no child protection plan (26%).

The conditions set included restriction of contact with particular individuals or requirements that the child attend medical check-ups, school or day nursery or that parents or children receive appropriate treatment for emotional, mental health or drug or alcohol problems. Conditions were often specified in a written agreement (54%) and were usually enforced at least partially (80%), that is to say, the family were generally challenged if it was discovered that they were not adhering to the conditions. It was made clear to some families (19%) that failure to comply with the conditions or the failure of the return would mean that the children returned permanently to care, whilst for a few (8%), compliance with conditions meant that discharging the care order would be considered.

Support for the return

Services or support were provided to the majority of families (84% of those with open cases) to help them adhere to conditions or assist in the success of the return. Six per cent of the cases had been closed immediately on return. Support took several forms (see Table 7.2) and was often provided as a package, which included, for example, regular respite care, financial or material aid and domestic help. Ongoing specialist support or intervention was also often provided by mental health services or other agencies.

Two-fifths of the children's families (41%) received financial or material support either at the start of the return (13%) or on an ongoing basis (28%). This included payments for food or nappies or other household necessities or the provision of bedding or a cooker or other domestic equipment. The same proportion (41%) was assisted by a family support worker occasionally (10%) or weekly or more often (31%), who helped with household chores, childcare and general life skills. Frequently these family support workers helped families over and over again with the same tasks.

Support with child care was also frequently provided. A quarter of the

Table 7.2
Support provided by children's services during the return

	% of open cases (n = 169 except where shown)
Domestic	
Financial/material support	41%
Family support worker	41%
Transport	34%
Childcare	
Respite care	24%
Play-scheme/activity group	12%
Childminding/nursery for pre-school children (n = 52)	57%
Support worker for school-age children (n = 115)	11%
Direct work	
With parents	20%
With children	19%
Total supported (in one or more of these ways)	84%

children were regularly or occasionally looked after in respite care during the return and a tenth (12%) attended play-schemes or other activity groups paid for by children's services. Where children were under school age, over half (57%) received regular day care in the form of childminding or nursery school. Whilst a quarter of these children were able to continue at the same day care facility they had attended when they were looked after, the remainder had to start in a new setting.

With children who attended school the proportions were reversed, with three-quarters (74%) continuing at the same school and only a quarter (26%) starting immediately at a new school. For these children other support, such as an adolescent support worker or young person's adviser (11%), was occasionally provided by children's services or another agency (e.g. Barnardo's) during the course of the return, and children's services also quite often (34%) provided or paid for transport for a time so that the children could finish a year or term in their current school.

Social workers also provided direct work to one in five of the children and parents. Over half of the children's parents (51%) were supported by children's services in more than one of these ways, including a quarter (25%) who were supported in more than two (for example, they were provided with financial aid, childminding and respite care). A third had only one form of support. This could be as little as a one-off financial payment or domestic support for just a week or two. Families whose circumstances had been assessed prior to the return, or who had children subject to court orders, received significantly more forms of support than where this did not apply.

During the course of the return, almost half of the parents (46%) and over two-fifths (43%) of the children aged four or more were also provided with specialist support by mental health teams (including mental health services for 31% of parents and 30% of children in open cases), probation, youth offending teams, community drug and alcohol services, local family centres, paediatricians, other health professionals (e.g. enuresis consultants) or specialist advisers (e.g. debt counsellors). These interventions usually focused on addressing particular issues or behaviours in a structured manner.

Parents were helped to address their own adversities, such as:

domestic violence, marital difficulties, mental health problems or previous abuse (10%); improve their parenting skills (9%); manage their children's behaviour (7%); work on the parent–child relationship (6%); reduce or abstain from drugs or alcohol (5%); manage their finances (2%); improve their confidence (2%); received specialist support for other reasons (9%); or to learn how to protect their child or manage their anger (1%). Almost a quarter of parents (23%) received help with more than one of these, most often a combination of work on their own adversities and child management. It was striking that whilst almost half (46%) of the mothers and a fifth (17%) of the fathers to whom the children returned had known drug or alcohol problems, only 5 per cent were provided with specific interventions or treatment to help them address their substance misuse.

Much of this work was a continuation of work started prior to the return and, as with services provided at that time, was significantly linked to the presence of assessment prior to return. The same was not true for the children, however, with only slightly more children (45% compared with 40%) receiving specialist services after assessment. This could be because these services tended to focus on addressing current (and therefore not necessarily predictable) needs such as problems with behaviour or anger (8%), school attendance (6%), substance misuse (1%), the parent–child relationship (1%), reactions to previous adversities (4%) or several of these (23%), or it could be because the policy of some providers (particularly CAMHS) was not to offer a service until the child was settled, which in some cases never happened. This meant that some of the most damaged or disruptive children were left without any specialist interventions.

A further 17 per cent of children and 24 per cent of parents were referred for specialist services during the return but did not receive a service, usually because they failed to turn up for appointments (62% of referred parents and 65% of similarly referred children), but sometimes because the service was not available or the outcome of the referral was not clear from the file (38% of parents and 35% of children).

Social workers may have worked directly with children to help them resolve or address their emotional or behavioural problems but this was not usually identified as a focus of direct work. Instead, documented direct work with children (19%) tended to focus on staying safe, getting on with siblings or resolving issues at school. Direct work with parents by the social workers (20%), however, frequently concentrated on managing the children's behaviour but also focused on improving the parent–child relationship or protecting the children from harm. It did not usually replicate any specialist support the parent was receiving; for example, a parent could be referred to a specialist drug and alcohol agency for help with their substance misuse while the social worker advised on behaviour management. However, families receiving more forms of support from children's services were also more likely to be in receipt of services from other agencies.

This may have been because where children were subject to care or supervision orders families were significantly more likely to be provided with more forms of support from children's services during the return (97% of these families received additional forms of support compared with 74% of families where children were not on orders) and were also somewhat more likely to be referred to other agencies. Interestingly, families of children subject to orders were more likely than others to receive financial or material support, day care and help with transport.

The same was not true for children subject to child protection plans, where only more specialist support for parents coincided with this disposition (61% of parents whose children were subject to child protection plans were receiving specialist services compared with 40% of parents whose children were not).

The other major source of formal support to families was the local authority, which provided educational assistance to over half (51%, 115) of the school-age children. Over a third received support from a classroom assistant in mainstream school, a tenth attended special school or a special unit within a mainstream school, and almost the same proportion were referred to "Behaviour Support" or seen by a school nurse or counsellor because of their emotional or behavioural problems. A few school-age children were not in school and remained without educational provision or received home tuition.

Informal support during the returns could be critical and was provided to over half of the children's families (52%) by friends, family or other organisations such as the church or Alcoholics Anonymous. Grandparents (15%) and other adult relatives (15%) were a key source of support, followed by friends (11%), siblings (2%) and members of organisations (2%). A few parents were supported by more than one person (7%). The level of support provided was rated as high or very high in the majority of cases (58%) and researcher ratings indicated that, in two-fifths of the cases (40%) the returns were only viable because of this informal support.

Whilst the relationship between informal and formal support was not clear cut, parents in receipt of the most forms of support from children's services and/or specialist services also tended to receive the most informal support (see also Quinton, 2004; Farmer et al, 2004). This may have reflected their ability to ask for and receive help or may simply reflect the fact that sources of informal support were more likely to be noted where there were greater concerns about the family.

Adequacy of the support provided during the return

In the previous chapter, researcher ratings suggested that, on the basis of the support packages proposed prior to the returns, only half (52%) of the families would be adequately resourced and supported such that the returns had a reasonable chance of success. In reality, the support that was provided during the returns was later rated as having been good or very good for three-fifths of the children's families (59%) and fair for a further quarter (28%). Indeed, in almost a third of the cases (31%), it was considered that intensive support from children's services (15%), other agencies (8%) or both (8%) sustained the returns for as long as they lasted. This is somewhat less than was the case for informal support. Families with children subject to court orders received significantly better support, with over three-quarters (77%) of it rated by the researchers as good or very good, compared with under half (45%) of the support provided to accommodated children. This was not true, however, for families of children subject to child protection plans.

Moreover, evidence of particularly highly competent social work (defined as being consistent and purposeful work with the child and the parents which helped to maintain the viability of the return, including regular monitoring of the child's progress to ensure the appropriateness of the placement) was evident in a fifth of cases (19%).

However, despite these apparently high levels of support, researcher ratings indicated that (in an ideal world) three-quarters of the children and their families (77%) would have benefited from additional support, particularly with ongoing substance misuse, health or mental health problems, the child's difficult behaviour, childcare responsibilities or domestic duties. These ratings, made with the benefit of hindsight, highlight the need for ongoing assessment of the family's circumstances as the full extent of many of these issues often did not become apparent until after the return had broken down (see Helen's story).

Helen's story

There had been concerns about Tara's parenting since the birth of her second child, Helen, but no thorough assessment of the home circumstances had been undertaken when, later that year, Tara asked for the girls to be accommodated whilst she went into hospital. They were then returned on the first day of a phased return despite the social worker noting that Tara seemed chaotic and low. Over the next four weeks, there were two social work visits, in one of which access to the home was denied. Tara also denied access to the health visitor, did not take up any family support services and did not answer phone calls. She subsequently called the social worker and admitted that she was not coping, that she was on drugs and in debt and had come very close to physically abusing the children, as a result of which the children were accommodated again.

It is also important to note that during the return almost a fifth of the parents (17%) and two-fifths of the children (40%) did not receive any support – either from children's services or a specialist agency – and many of the parents and children who did, experienced discontinuity of support because of changes of social worker or case closure.

Assessment during the return

Where the case was not immediately closed after reunification (94% of cases), assessment of the child and family circumstances occurred during the return in a quarter of cases. Two-fifths (40%) of the assessments were core assessments, the same proportion were expert assessments, with a small proportion (20%) of both. Assessment was significantly more likely to occur where there had already been an assessment of the family's circumstances prior to the return or if the child was subject to a child protection plan (40% of children on a plan were assessed compared with 18% of those who were not), suggesting that these children were the focus of considerable concern and/or monitoring. On the other hand, the circumstances of a third of children (33%) were never assessed, either prior to or during the return.

The parents' views of the start of the returns

Parents varied in how they described the beginning of their children's return home. Some reported a "honeymoon period" during which things went well at first, before reverting to how they had been. A few reported that they had been able to build on the improvements from the period in care, such as a two-and-a-half-year-old who returned from foster care to his mother out of nappies, with a bedtime and mealtime routine.

A few parents spoke of the need for their children to build up trust in them again and one mother of an eight-month-old baby said that her baby had not seemed close to her and had not slept well for the first few weeks until he settled. Some parents expressed joy at the children's return:

We just walked in and we were all back together.

Other parents said that the children were difficult from the start and that 'nothing had changed' or new difficult behaviours had emerged, especially as children reached adolescence.

A few mothers commented that overnight stays had not prepared them for the difficult behaviour their children showed once they returned home full time (see also Farmer and Parker, 1991):

Weekends at home had not prepared me for how difficult he would be.

One mother explained that she had mollycoddled her son and 'wrapped him in cotton wool' because he had been sexually abused while in care. However, she had made a rod for her own back as he returned to being hard to control.

The mothers who were discharged into the community with their babies from mother and baby placements or residential assessment or treatment centres were generally happy to be there and this may reflect the fact that the timing of these returns was carefully considered. Other parents and some children, as we have seen, felt that the returns had occurred too soon. Whilst many children were pleased to be home, in a few cases they were not.

The parents' views of monitoring and assessment during the return

The parents' views of the monitoring of their children were variable. Only 11 of the 34 parents said that the children were monitored or assessed during the return. Interestingly, the parents of seven of the children who were on court orders did not consider that the children had been monitored.

Some parents accepted being subject to monitoring more readily than others. One mother, who was disillusioned because she thought that her account of the family situation had been ignored in favour of what her mother (the children's grandmother) had said, described being monitored as follows:

They used to get you talking and know all your business: where you were going, what you were doing every day like. Well, I want out of this. I don't want to know.

The parents' views of the support provided for the return are described in detail in Chapter 9 when we look at their views of the returns.

We look now at the children's accounts of their experiences when they went home.

The children's experience of continuity and change

The families

For the five children we interviewed whose parents had a new partner or were no longer living with a former partner, three children had mixed feelings about these changes and two were positive. As we see later, relationships with their mothers' partners were sometimes seen by children as an important negative or positive influence on their returns. There were changes in the children in the family for five children, of whom one found this negative, two had mixed feelings and two were positive. Six children returned to other changes such as a different house, a different bedroom or very different routines, with a range of views as to whether this was positive or negative.

For example, Jardine returned to her stepfather, who was dealing drugs, and to a chaotic household. She had liked the routine of foster care with bedtimes, mealtimes and regular school attendance but once with her stepfather she 'missed loads of school' as no one got her up in the morning. Indeed, sometimes she was left alone in the house for long periods. Sophie had to adjust to sharing her home with the two new children born as a result of her mother's new relationship and she was initially jealous of them. Carrie returned after her father came out of prison:

> *It felt weird when I got back. It took a few weeks to get used to family routine again and feeling that you do have a place.*

Tina too found fitting back into the family difficult:

> *The rest of the family had got used to me not being there, so it was sort of, like, I was an outsider, sort of, even though I was family. I was like an outsider because I hadn't been there.*

Worse still, she had a new bedroom:

> *That's the bit I didn't like. I went home and none of my stuff was where I left it . . . All my stuff had been shared out. Paul [the younger brother] had all my furniture and Suzie had all my stuff, so I had nothing apart from the stuff I took with me . . . I hated it.*

These findings about the additional difficulties of adapting back when changes had been made in children's absence echo those from previous research (Bullock *et al*, 1993).

School

Most of the children we interviewed returned to the same school (14), although six of them had mixed feelings or were negative about this, whilst of the three who changed school when they went home, one was positive.

Schools provided considerable support for these children during reunification as we will see and in at least two cases appeared to be crucial to success. Some children were managing at school, on occasion as a result of classroom support, but others were struggling, disliked school or began to truant. For example, Tina hated school, was picked on in class, struggled with the work and rarely attended. In fact, she was dyslexic and needed specialist help. She started to alienate her friends and became a loner.

Friends

Two young people had not been able to keep up with their friends whilst away, but others had maintained contact with some or all of their friends. However, four children reported having no close friends and five, only one or two close friends during the return. Eight were able to confide in their friends but 10 could not. Two of the children reported being bullied and picked on by other children.

The children's worries about the returns and confiding

Most of the children had been worried about how the return would work out. They were often concerned that previous difficulties would recur, in particular that their behaviour would deteriorate, that they would not get on with their parents, or that a parent's drinking would resume or mental illness reach crisis point. Jason was aged 14 when he went to live with his father, who had physically abused him in the past. His anxiety, though, focused on his brother:

I was a bit wary about moving into my dad's because my older brother, Jim, has put me down all my life.

One boy was 'very nervous' that his father's second marriage would end in the same way as his first, with domestic violence leading to him going into care. Indeed, several children were anxious that they might have to return to care again. Tracey had not thought that her mother would want her back because she was so naughty and was worried that she would be 'thrown out again'. Another girl said:

I worried that I'd return to care and never be able to go home again.

Their worries about returning home were fully or partially borne out for 13 of the children, whilst six others had encountered additional unexpected problems. The children had also nurtured hopes of how reunification would work. The return did work out as nine of the young people had hoped, but this was only partially true for five of them and the hopes of five children were not met.

In spite of the extent of their worries, seven of the young people said that they had confided in no one during the return. Other children (11) had confided, most often in friends but also occasionally with a mother, siblings or teachers or in more than one of these. Some had also been able to confide in their social workers, although they sometimes had reservations about doing so, as we will see later.

Children's views of support and services for their returns

The young people described a wide variety of services to assist them during the returns.

Contact with social workers

Six children said that they had seen their social workers about the right amount, others too little or too much, but five saw them rarely or not at all. Ten of the children had found their social worker fairly or very helpful, although five had not (of whom two had seen little of their workers). Ten of the children confided in their social workers sometimes or a lot, whilst seven did not.

Several children expressed reservations about confiding in their social workers, explaining that they did not trust them not to share their confidences with their parents or foster carers and that this could get them into trouble, and in one case, a young person said that she had been beaten up as a result of a confidence betrayed. One child had been warned by her mother not to trust the social worker. She said:

> *I don't speak to her [the social worker], because they speak to my mum . . . Because she said that she wouldn't tell anybody and everything, but social workers normally tell different social workers and then they tell the school and everything . . . I don't want her telling anybody.*

Two young people said either that social workers had made things worse by betraying a confidence or that they disliked them. For example, when Jardine's stepfather came out of prison, she absconded to live with him at the age of 12, even though there had been no assessment of the suitability of this arrangement. The file recorded that she was left alone for long periods and that the stepfather was using and dealing drugs and that Jardine began drinking and smoking cannabis. Jardine remembered seeing the social worker only once, when the social worker warned Jardine about her truancy, and she saw the worker's additional efforts to monitor the situation at home as intrusive:

> *I'm not bothered about seeing social workers because she was snotty, like. She was always on your back saying, 'Oh, so what is going on at home then? Do you think there's any drugs going at home? Do you think this? Do you think that? Do you think this?' Couldn't talk to her. I didn't like the social worker really.*

She saw social workers as people who took you into care and would not confide in them. In fact, the social worker had only been able to gain access to the house three times in spite of many attempts to visit and the case was then unallocated and later closed.

In contrast, Chris's social worker took him out for chats and was 'brilliant' and also gave his mother back-up. Sheila found her social worker helpful:

He took me out and made me smile.

Lindy had also found her social worker helpful but had wanted help from the social worker to improve her relationship with her mother. She said she would have liked:

. . . help with the family. 'Cos they all turned their back on me, just didn't want to know.

Schools

Thirteen children considered that their school had been supportive of their return, although only 10 (just over half) had found the school really helpful. A number of children mentioned feeling close to a teacher at school, some of whom had given them special help. Chris, for example, was enthusiastic about his Year Head. She became his mentor and confidante, gave him a great deal of support and got him involved in drama and with the Duke of Edinburgh's Award scheme. He talked to her a lot and she would suggest what she might have done in situations similar to those Chris faced:

She's a star . . . She helps me get through things and she's my mentor.

This teacher appeared to have been a key influence on the success of Chris' return.

Professional or other help

During the interviews, the young people also mentioned receiving help from psychiatrists, counsellors, an art therapist, support workers or Connexions advisers, leaving care workers, a young people's adviser, a mentor and respite carers. One young person described respite care thus:

That was wicked that was. I loved it there.

Of the eight young people who saw health or mental health professionals, most saw them as helpful or very helpful, although three did not.

Sheila, who saw a counsellor and an art therapist, commented that neither had helped her to get close to her mother. Josie had received counselling at CAMHS, which she had found helpful, but said that she had had few friends at school and was bullied and was not sleeping well. Jason found sessions with a therapist brought back too many memories and was too painful so he stopped attending, whilst Jamie had refused his social worker's referral to a psychologist: 'It's all a load of crap'. He found psychiatric involvement 'not helpful'.

In addition, two of the children maintained contact with their former foster carers who provided support and with whom the child, in one case, got on better than with her mother.

The social workers' accounts of visits to the families

Following the children's return home, the social workers set up a pattern of visiting the family. However, the length of time that social work visiting continued was variable and some cases were closed within a few months of the child's return home without the problems having been resolved, including at least one case where there were substantial concerns about the children's welfare.

Two social workers visited infrequently or not at all because the parents refused access. In one case, the social worker did not visit after she was refused entry by the parents, who made a complaint about her practice. In a second case, the social worker visited weekly for the first few weeks, but the parents then avoided visits, so the social worker then visited only occasionally and rarely saw the child even though she was on a care order and there were continuing difficulties in the mother–child relationship.

Social work with parents and children

Following the child's return home, the social workers in 10 of the interview cases were engaged in work with parents which focused on parent–child relationships, management of the child's behaviour and the parents' self-esteem and self-confidence. In several cases, their work also involved responding to crises related to alcohol and drug use, violence, risks to the children and children who went missing. Sometimes the social workers were mainly co-ordinating work undertaken by other professionals, including family support workers. In five of these cases social workers were also involved in work with the children.

Other services

In six cases, social workers said that foster carers maintained contact with the children following their return home and provided support to the families; the foster carers also provided respite care for four of the children. This was described as a key factor in supporting the return home for three of them. In contrast, residential carers did not maintain contact with any of the children who returned home from residential care.

Other forms of support and packages of services were provided to the parents of 12 children and these were seen as very useful, even though in some cases they were not sufficient to sustain the return home. The packages of support services included some or all of the following: respite care; day care; specialist help on parent–child relationships or with children's behaviour (from CAMHS); specialist help with parental confidence or self-esteem (through a family centre); help with budgeting and financial support; assistance from a family support worker; psychiatric treatment; family therapy; and involvement in a parenting programme.

Services were also provided to children in nine of the families, including: specialist help with their behaviour or anger management; psychotherapy, psychiatric treatment and family therapy; and help from mentors or befrienders, a youth offending team worker and a Young Carers Project. In addition, nine children had help with their school attendance or additional educational assistance. Schools were sometimes able to provide help when contact with other professionals had been refused. However, in three cases, no work was undertaken with the parents or child, because the parents refused contact with social workers and other professionals.

When asked whether there were other services that they thought the families had needed, six social workers mentioned a variety of services that parents had declined, including help with alcoholism, drug use, a parent's previous abuse and violence. In addition, some (5) families were described as socially isolated, without support from family or friends, and this issue later emerged as important to return outcomes.

Now that the parents', children's and social workers' experiences at the start of reunification have been described, we turn in the next chapter to examine the progress of the returns.

Summary

- Two-thirds of the children (64%) returned to the same parents (or parent figures) they had lived with previously, a quarter (26%) returned to households a parent or partner had moved out from or into since they were looked after, and a tenth returned to a different parent.
- Only half of the children (52%) had not experienced any changes in their household membership when they were returned.
- Three-quarters of the children in the case file sample were returned to parents who were thought to have previously maltreated them, slightly more (82%) to parents with a history of domestic violence, drug or alcohol misuse or prostitution/open use of pornography (or a combination of these) and three-fifths to mothers or fathers with mental health problems. Ten per cent of the mothers either had learning difficulties or physical health problems or disabilities.
- Two-fifths (42%) returned to parents who had demonstrated ambivalence about parenting them and a third of the children (37%) had been unsuccessfully returned to these carers before.
- Support was provided by children's services to the majority of the children's families (84%) to assist in the success of the returns. Almost half of the parents (46%) and over two-fifths (43%) of the children (aged four or over) were also provided with specialist support by other agencies.
- Whilst almost half of the mothers and a fifth of the fathers to whom the children returned had drug or alcohol problems, only five per cent received any treatment for this.
- Families with children under care or supervision orders were more likely than others to be supported by other agencies, provided with more forms of support from children's services, and were more often

subject to conditions and monitoring by other professionals, such as health visitors or paediatricians.

- Over half of the school-age children also received additional support from the local education authority. Family, friends and members of organisations such as Alcoholics Anonymous also provided support to over half of the children's families.
- Researcher ratings indicated that three-quarters of all the children and their families would have benefited from additional support. Almost a fifth of the parents (17%) and two-fifths of the children (40%) did not receive any support – either from children's services or a specialist agency – during the return.
- Almost half (48%) the cases had been closed before the end of the two-year follow-up period. Many (47%) had been closed despite ongoing concerns and most (70%) of such cases had to be re-opened.
- The circumstances of a third of the children (33%) were never assessed either prior to or during the return.

Parent, child and social worker perceptions of going home

- Some parents accepted being subject to monitoring more readily than others. They reported very variable experiences of the start of the returns, from those who were able to build on improvements from the period in care to others where difficulties continued as soon as children returned to them.
- The children we interviewed reacted to changes in their families and home circumstances in different ways. Some were pleased and others unhappy when a parent's new partner or new children joined the household. Changes of house or of bedroom could make the adjustment more difficult, with a few children feeling like outsiders in their own families. More than half the children had found their school very helpful during the return.
- Most of the children we interviewed had been worried about how the return would work out and a third of them had confided in no one during the return.
- More than half of the children said that they had found their social workers helpful and the same proportion had confided in them.

- The social workers who were interviewed described some quite complex packages of support that had been provided for the children and their parents; where no work had been undertaken, this was generally because parents refused services. Six (27%) of the foster carers (in the social work interview sample) had maintained contact with the children after their return home and provided support to their families, sometimes including respite care.

8 The children's progress at home

This chapter describes the progress of the children after they went home, examining their school attendance and progress, emotional or behavioural problems and how often they were exposed to parental substance misuse, domestic violence or child abuse or neglect. The parents', children's and social workers' reflections on the children's progress at home are reported in the next chapter.

Parental behaviours during the return

Some parental behaviours showed a great deal of improvement on return. Domestic violence, which was a feature of two-thirds (67%) of the families before the children entered care, was reported in under a fifth (16%) during the two-year follow-up period. Substance misuse declined from being an issue for 59 per cent of families to 32 per cent and inappropriate sexual activity (such as prostitution or the open use of pornography) from 15 per cent to three per cent, as shown in Table 8.1.

However, the difficulties facing practitioners are shown by the recurrence rates for these issues, that is, if a specific behaviour had occurred previously, how often it occurred again during the return. Whilst domestic violence and inappropriate sexual activity were recorded as recurring in only 21% and 18% of the families respectively within the two-year follow-up period (or the end of the return if sooner), drugs misuse recurred in two-fifths (42%) and alcohol misuse in as many as half (51%) of the families, as shown in Table 8.2.

The lower recurrence rates for domestic violence and inappropriate sexual activity may have been because often the parent who had shown this behaviour had left the family. The recurrence rates for alcohol and drugs misuse, on the other hand, may have been because parents had insufficient motivation to tackle their substance misuse and/or inadequate support to do so – only five per cent of parents were supported by drugs or alcohol professionals as we have seen. Often social workers believed that parents had stopped drinking or using drugs (or moderated their use

Table 8.1

Incidence of parental behaviours before and after the children were looked after

	Percentage of families (n = 141)	
	Before	After
Domestic violence	**67%**	**16%**
Domestic violence only	19%	4%
Domestic violence & substance misuse	36%	11%
Domestic violence & concerning sexual activity	1%	0%
Domestic violence, substance misuse & concerning sexual activity	11%	1%
Substance misuse	**59%**	**32%**
Substance misuse only	11%	19%
Substance misuse & domestic violence	36%	11%
Substance misuse & concerning sexual activity	1%	1%
Substance misuse, domestic violence & concerning sexual activity	11%	1%
Concerning sexual activity	**15%**	**3%**
Concerning sexual activity only	2%	1%
Concerning sexual activity & domestic violence	1%	0%
Concerning sexual activity & substance misuse	1%	1%
Concerning sexual activity, domestic violence & substance misuse	11%	1%

Table 8.2

Recurrence rates for parental behaviours

	Percentage of families (n = 141)
Alcohol misuse	51%
Drugs misuse	42%
Domestic violence	21%
Concerning sexual activity	18%

sufficiently) before the children were returned, when they had not. Usually workers had simply taken the parent's word for it, with only one mother required to provide a negative drug test, conducted by a drug treatment agency. There seemed to be a lack of understanding about substance misuse (or an inaccurate assessment as to the extent of the problem) such that many social workers expected parents to be able to moderate or stop their drinking or drug use with little or no intervention. In fact, the high recurrence rates for substance misuse highlight the difficulties facing parents with these problems and suggest the need for a greater use of available services and interventions and even (following in the footsteps of the criminal justice system) mandatory drug or alcohol testing of parents with substance misuse issues, where necessary (see also Harris, 2008).

Parental behaviours and adversities which were associated with parental substance misuse

This point is very important as a number of other adverse parental behaviours occurred significantly more often when substance misuse was present (see Table 8.3). These were domestic violence and poor parenting skills, which included inconsistent or unresponsive parenting, aggressive discipline or a marked lack of warmth towards the child. This was also true of parental anti-social behaviour (including damage to property and conflict with neighbours) and marked instability, characterised by multiple parental partners or house moves or by a very chaotic and unpredictable environment for the child.

Table 8.3
Substance misuse during the return and parental behaviours

Parental behaviours	*Percentage of families*		
	Substance misuse (n = 44)	*No substance misuse (n = 97)*	*Statistically significant at p<0.001*
Poor parenting skills	82%	41%	Yes
Marked instability	70%	14%	Yes
Anti-social behaviour	59%	4%	Yes
Domestic violence	36%	7%	Yes

In addition, some social adversities, specifically, poor home conditions, financial problems and social isolation, all occurred more often when parents had drug or alcohol problems (see Table 8.4). This is not surprising since obtaining the substance of choice often becomes the most compelling thing in the life of the alcoholic or drug addict to the detriment of family relationships and the home.

Table 8.4
Substance misuse during the return and social/environmental adversities

| Social/environmental adversity | Percentage of families | | Significance levels |
	Substance misuse (n = 44)	No substance misuse (n = 97)	
Poor home conditions	43%	13%	p < 0.001
Financial problems	54%	19%	p < 0.001
Social isolation	32%	16%	p < 0.05

Child abuse or neglect during the return

In total, there were concerns that almost half of the children (46%) had suffered abuse or neglect during the return – half the number who were thought to have been maltreated prior to becoming looked after (91%). Whilst a 50 per cent reduction in the overall incidence of maltreatment is substantial, recurrence rates remained fairly high (see Table 8.5), particularly for neglect (33%), emotional abuse (25%) and physical abuse (21%). The lower rates for sexual abuse may have been because some of the perpetrators were from outside the family.

We found that three-fifths (60%) of all the alleged child abuse or neglect that occurred during the return was perpetrated by substance misusing parents, 78 per cent of whom were thought to have maltreated their children during the return, compared with only 29 per cent of parents without substance misuse problems. This difference was highly significant. All types of abuse and neglect occurred significantly more often where drug or alcohol misuse was evident (see Table 8.6). Maltreatment was especially common where parents misused drugs (with 93% of

Table 8.5

Incidence of abuse or neglect before and after the children were looked after and recurrence rates

| | Percentage of children (n = 180) | | Recurrence rates |
	Incidence before	Incidence after	
Neglect	68%	24%	33%
Physical abuse	61%	20%	21%
Emotional abuse	61%	18%	25%
Sexual abuse	28%	4%	9%
Any form of maltreatment	91%	46%	50%

Table 8.6

Substance misuse during the return and child abuse or neglect

| Child maltreatment | Percentage of families | | Significance levels |
	Substance misuse (n = 44)	No substance misuse (n = 97)	
Neglect	55%	8%	p < 0.001
Physical abuse	33%	13%	p < 0.01
Sexual abuse	8%	2%	p < 0.05
Emotional abuse	32%	12%	p < 0.01
Any abuse or neglect	78%	29%	p < 0.001

children in these families suffering abuse or neglect compared with 75% of children of parents who misused alcohol).

New occurrences of suspected abuse or neglect were relatively rare except when it came to physical abuse (there was one new occurrence of sexual abuse, three of neglect, six of emotional abuse but 13 of physical abuse), and so it follows that previous maltreatment significantly predicted further similar maltreatment during the return for all forms of abuse or neglect except physical abuse.

A number of other factors were significantly associated with abuse and neglect during the returns. Some of these were also associated with parental substance misuse, such as parental anti-social behaviour, domestic violence, reported financial problems, instability, poor home conditions and poor parenting skills. Other factors were maternal mental health problems, the child having experienced multiple previous adversities and prior professional concerns about the return (see Table 8.7). Further statistical analysis using logistic regression revealed that poor parenting skills were the greatest predictor of child maltreatment during the return (possibly because of elements of overlap in the definitions of poor parenting skills, emotional abuse and physical abuse i.e. emotional abuse includes a marked lack of warmth and physical abuse includes aggressive over-chastisement, both of which would also rate as poor parenting skills), followed by drug misuse and then alcohol misuse, which together accounted for 50 per cent of the variance.

Slightly fewer children who were subject to a court order or who had been assessed before return or had received adequate support were abused or neglected, but these differences were not significant. Levels of

Table 8.7
Factors associated with child abuse or neglect

	Percentage of children maltreated		
	Where factor present	Where factor not present	Significance level
Drugs misuse	93%	37%	p<0.001
Anti-social behaviour	81%	35%	p<0.001
Domestic violence	79%	40%	p<0.001
Instability	76%	33%	p<0.001
Alcohol misuse	75%	38%	p<0.001
Poor home conditions	74%	37%	p<0.001
Poor parenting skills	71%	17%	p<0.001
Financial problems	63%	37%	p<0.001
Maternal mental health problems	59%	31%	p<0.001
Prior multiple adversities (>4)	53%	36%	p < 0.05
Prior professional concerns about the return	60%	39%	p < 0.05

maltreatment were at similar levels whether or not children were subject to child protection plans or returned home during care proceedings.

The majority of the alleged abuse was by the birth parents, particularly birth mothers (62%) either alone (43%) or with a partner (19%). Birth fathers alone were responsible for a tenth of the suspected abuse and occasionally (3%) with their partners. Stepfathers were the next largest group of perpetrators, responsible for six per cent of the alleged abuse and more rarely people outside the family, such as grandparents (1%) or lodgers (1%) for the remainder.

Fifteen per cent of the children were thought to have been abused by more than one of these people (e.g. by a parent and grandparent). These figures were relatively consistent across all the different forms of maltreatment with slightly more physical abuse by stepfathers (and less by birth mothers) and sexual abuse perpetrated only by relatives or others outside the household. In over a third of the families (38%) where the child had siblings at home concerns had also been recorded about possible abuse or neglect of them too.

What happened after children were abused or neglected?

In the majority of cases (62%) the children remained with the suspected abuser/s after concerns had been raised, although in 10 per cent of cases one or both of the alleged abusers left the household and in 17 per cent of cases the children were immediately taken back into care or otherwise removed from the household. The rest of the time either the alleged perpetrator did not live in the household (6%) or their whereabouts were not clear (5%).

Much of the time (59%) the decision for the child to remain at home was appropriate, as either the maltreatment was not severe enough to warrant removal or was by someone who had left or was outside the family. One of the most severe cases of physical abuse, for example, was meted out by school bullies, who assaulted and burned a teenage girl and threatened to kill her. Some of the cases of sexual abuse were also perpetrated by other young people or those outside the extended family. In other cases, innovative responses to the parental difficulties enabled the children to remain at home. Safe house arrangements, for example, were set up for one girl enabling her to receive sufficient care when her mother (whose parenting was otherwise adequate) had an episode of binge drinking. Many of these returns did, however, subsequently break down.

Sometimes (41%), however, children appeared to have remained at home inappropriately, for too long, or without sufficient intervention or investigation of the alleged maltreatment (see also Farmer and Lutman, 2009; Ward *et al*, 2010). Seven children, for example, told neighbours, teachers or their social worker that they had been hit (two with objects) but, without further evidence, little resulted from these disclosures. In the most severe case, a child described being punched, kicked and hit by his mother but these allegations were not investigated, possibly because of cultural barriers. Twenty-one other children remained at home (either for the whole two-year follow-up period or for a substantial period of time) despite ongoing concerns. Two suffered recurring non-accidental injuries, two, repeat sexual abuse and 17, ongoing neglect or emotional abuse (see for example, Rose and Hugh's story). Most of the children in these circumstances were older, but some were young. One girl, for example, was only three when she suffered facial injuries on two separate occasions and then bruising after an object had been thrown at her. Two of these incidents resulted in child protection investigations but no further action, despite 11 phone calls to police and three to children's services expressing concerns about her welfare during the same period.

Often the delay in returning the children to care occurred because of lengthy care proceedings where a return was being attempted or because there was thought to be insufficient evidence to initiate care proceedings or to remove the children, and social workers considered that they simply had to wait for an incident (or further incident) to occur before they were able to act to protect the children. One boy, for example, returned home at the age of 14 to drug-dealing parents and immediately there were concerns about his own drug use and non-attendance at school. Eight months later, the family were evicted from their home after the father was arrested for drug-related offences. However, the boy refused to be accommodated and as there was not felt to be sufficient grounds to place him in a secure unit, he did not return to care until he was arrested for several offences and remanded to a secure unit by the court. In all, there were 15 children (8%) whose return to care was not sufficiently timely (as in this case) and 13 (7%) who remained at home at the end of the two-year follow-up period when researchers thought they should have been removed.

Where children did return to care more swiftly (17%), often the children or parents requested care after incidents of abuse or neglect, either because of a breakdown in the parent–child relationship or because the parents were fearful of causing further harm. At other times, children (mostly under the age of six) were removed after contact with the police or medical services following incidents of maltreatment or criminal activity. In the most severe cases, children were threatened by parents under the influence of drugs or alcohol, or sustained repeated injuries which their parents could not adequately explain.

Rose and Hugh's story

Rose and Hugh's parents both had moderate learning difficulties and the children were made subject to a child protection plan on more than one occasion due to continuing concerns about inadequate supervision, poor home conditions, and their mother's relationships with men who had offended against children. As there had been no sustained improvement in the situation despite many attempts at support, care proceedings were initiated. Both children were noted to wet their beds and have serious behavioural problems. Therapeutic intervention was provided for the children and they were made subject to one-year supervision orders. The parents co-operated only sporadically with the support provided, the children were neglected, and their well-being deteriorated again. Police reports about the home environment subsequently triggered further care proceedings, which had not concluded at the end of the follow-up period when the children were still at home.

Monitoring of the children during the return

Despite the difficulties in the families to which the children had returned, and the abuse that the children experienced, only just over a quarter (28%) of them were subject to a child protection plan during the return and this included under a third (30%) of the children who had been maltreated. For three-fifths (58%) of the children on child protection plans, these were discontinued during the return (including 12 children who were maltreated during that time). Researcher ratings indicated that a fifth of the children were inadequately monitored despite clear reasons for continuing concern and, as might be expected, most of these children were not on child protection plans.

Without adequate monitoring in place for many children, researcher ratings indicated that (from the information available on file) a clear picture of the child's safety and progress could not be obtained in a quarter (26%) of the open cases, with these children monitored too infrequently or without sufficient clarity to be sure about their welfare. In addition, almost half (47%) of the children aged five or over did not appear to have been given adequate opportunity to express their feelings about the return to their social worker (or this had not been clearly recorded on the file).

The children's development during the return
With that in mind, it is worth noting that the information that follows may be an underestimate of the children's difficulties. As can be seen in Table 8.8, with the exception of sexualised behaviour and sexually abusive behaviour, all forms of behaviour were more likely to recur during the return than be resolved. So, for example, the recurrence rates during the returns included behaviour problems (42%), under-achievement at school (38%), conflict with parents (33%), being beyond control (33%), not attending school (32%), having emotional (31%) or peer problems (25%) and offending (23%).

A third of the children (33%) had shown new difficult behaviours by the end of the return (or two-year follow-up period). These were often behaviours which reflected the children's increasing ages such as offending behaviour (13%) and substance misuse (10%).

Quite high proportions of children showed challenging or worrying behaviours once home with their parents, including behaviour problems (46%), under-achievement (43%), non-attendance at school (42% of school-age children), poor attendance at nursery (40% of pre-schoolers), conflict with parents (37%), offending behaviour (36%) and emotional problems (34%). Whilst over two-fifths of the school-age children were

Table 8.8
Children's behaviour by the end of the return

Children's behaviour	Previously an issue & during the return (recurrence)	New issue	Cols 1 + 2 An issue during return	Previously an issue but not during the return (non-recurrence)
Emotional problems	31%	3%	**34%**	8%
Behaviour problems	42%	4%	**46%**	5%
Hyper-kinetic problems	16%	3%	**19%**	3%
Substance misuse	9%	10%	**19%**	3%
Offending	23%	13%	**36%**	8%
School non-attendance	32%	10%	**42%**	6%
School exclusion	12%	8%	**20%**	10%
School under-achievement	38%	5%	**43%**	5%
Attachment problems	13%	5%	**18%**	7%
Conflict with parents/carers	33%	4%	**37%**	4%
Conflict with siblings	22%	2%	**24%**	5%
Peer problems	25%	4%	**29%**	7%
Sexualised behaviour	5%	1%	**6%**	9%
High-risk relationships	17%	6%	**23%**	8%
Sexual abuse of others	0%	1%	**1%**	4%
Being beyond parental control	33%	3%	**36%**	7%

under-achieving at school (43%), only just over one-fifth (23%) had been issued with a Statement of Special Educational Needs, almost which would have provided services to help with their school work. In contrast, the children were usually well physically, with only a tenth (9%) often or frequently ill.

Overall, a fifth (18%) of the children were considered to have severe problems that needed remedial action and a third (29%) had serious problems that needed specialist interventions, with the remainder having no (33%) or only minor or transitory problems (20%). However, only a third of the children needing remedial action were receiving help, as were half of those requiring specialist interventions.

Despite the extent of their difficulties, most children (57%) appeared to be close to their parent/s, although a tenth (11%) were close to only one of couple carers and a worrying third (32%) were not close to either parent figure. Sibling relationships also appeared to be important, with almost three-quarters (72%) of the children who returned home to or with siblings appearing close to at least one brother or sister. However, of the third of children who were not close to any carer, most – a fifth (23%) of the whole sample – were not thought to have a significant attachment to any adults at all, leaving them very much alone in the world.

A third (30%) of the parents admitted that they were having difficulties with their children, with some (18%) demanding that their child return to care and others requesting that their home life remain under review. For a further quarter of parents (26%), there was evidence on file that they were ambivalent, unwilling or unable to care for their children adequately.

Onlookers frequently voiced their anxieties about the parents' care, and over the course of the returns, concerns were reported about as many as two-thirds (69%) of the children. These were flagged up predominantly by teachers (13%) but also by criminal justice professionals (8%), anonymous referrers (7%), health professionals (6%), friends, neighbours or kin (5%), other agencies (3%) or more than one of these (27%). Many of these concerns were raised about the issues that had originally led to the children going into care. These, in some cases, resulted in the instigation of fresh care proceedings.

Legal history of the children during the return

When they went home, almost 60 per cent of the children were discharged from care to their parents. The remaining children were returned home subject to supervision orders (4%), interim care orders (24%) or care orders (13%). Of these, in a third of cases the parents had been given explicit requirements to fulfil so that the orders be discharged or varied to an order of a lesser magnitude.

In relation to the cases where the children were subject to orders, for almost half (45%) there was no change in legal status and the original orders were continuing at the end of the return (or two-year follow-up period). In other cases, supervision orders, interim care orders and in one case, a care order, were discharged or allowed to expire, whilst a fifth of cases were varied from interim care orders to supervision orders. In another fifth of cases, supervision orders or interim care orders were converted into care orders and, in addition, for the 180 children, 30 new sets of care proceedings (17%) were initiated during the return (four after a previous order had expired, been discharged or varied), usually because children had been abused or neglected. All but one of these new care proceedings resulted in further orders by the end of the two-year follow-up period (14 care orders, eight interim care orders and seven supervision orders).

From the time of the returns, therefore, there was very little change overall in the number of children subject to orders (41% at the point of the return compared with 36% at the end of the two-year follow-up period – by which time a number of the supervision orders had expired) and no change in the number on remand or in secure accommodation (2%).

These figures, however, disguise the number of children whose returns broke down before the end of the two-year follow-up period and we look at this in Chapter 10.

The parents, children and social workers gave their views about what had helped to make the children's returns work or in contrast why they had failed. We consider these in the next chapter.

Summary

- Drug misuse recurred in two-fifths of families and alcohol misuse in over half, while domestic violence recurred in only a fifth.
- Recurrence rates were also high for social isolation (74%), financial problems (59%), poor parenting skills (57%), marked instability (53%), parental anti-social behaviour (43%) and poor home conditions (42%), despite a drop in the overall prevalence rates of these behaviours. All of these factors were significantly more likely to occur where a parent was misusing drugs or alcohol than where substance misuse was not an issue, as was domestic violence.
- Children of substance misusing parents (78%) were also much more likely to suffer incidents of abuse or neglect than children of parents

without substance misuse issues (29%). Maltreatment was more common where parents misused drugs (93%) than alcohol (75%).

- Overall, almost half of the children (46%) suffered abuse or neglect during the return, which was half the number who had been maltreated prior to being looked after (91%). Neglect (33%), emotional abuse (25%) and physical abuse (21%) were particularly likely to recur, whilst a recurrence of sexual abuse was relatively rare (9%).
- Logistic regression revealed that poor parenting skills were the greatest predictor of child maltreatment during the return, followed by parental drug misuse and alcohol misuse.
- Most children (62%) remained at home with the suspected abuser(s) after concerns had been raised, but 17 per cent were immediately removed from the household.
- Much of the time (59%) the decision for the child to remain at home was appropriate. Sometimes (41%), however, children appeared to have remained at home inappropriately, for too long, or without sufficient intervention or investigation of alleged maltreatment.
- Researcher ratings indicated that a fifth of the children were inadequately monitored despite clear ongoing reasons for concern.
- With the exception of sexualised behaviour and sexually abusive behaviour, all forms of difficult behaviour were more likely to recur during the return than remain a resolved issue. A third of the children also exhibited new difficult behaviour by the end of the return. There were fairly high levels of behavioural and emotional problems and other difficulties.
- Many parents struggled to cope with these behaviours. Concerns were reported about two-thirds (69%) of the children by education, health and other professionals, as well as by relatives and neighbours. A third of the children were not close to either parent figure.
- New care proceedings were instigated in almost one in five cases.

9 Parents', children's and social workers' views of the returns

Having reviewed the children's progress at home from the evidence on the case files, we look now at the parents', children's and social workers' views of the children's returns, how children got on and the support provided.

Of the returns to the 34 parents we interviewed, just under half (44%, 15) had been of good quality or "successful" and just over half (56%, 19) had not. Our ratings of the quality of the returns have been explained in Chapter 2 and in this chapter we use the term "successful" to describe good-quality returns and "unsuccessful" for those which were of borderline or poor quality.

Parents' views of successful returns

The interviews with parents revealed that there were a range of situations in which reunification was successful.

Returns after improvement in parental difficulties

Seven of the 15 successful returns (47%) discussed in the parent interviews were because of improvements in the parents' difficulties as a result of treatment, often accompanied by subsequent support.

Parental treatment

Two of the successful returns were clearly as a result of treatment provided for the mother prior to return. Julie's mother, for example, had had six months' treatment for her alcohol problems before Julie returned to her at the age of 12. This was the third time Julie had returned to her mother from care, but as a result of the treatment, her mother stayed sober except for occasional binge drinking, when Julie would often stay at home to support her mother. The return was made possible because Julie was considered old enough to look after herself if necessary and she also had a "safe house" to which she could go when her mother was drinking. Julie's mother also had considerable support from friends and family.

Similarly, Irena's mother, Mrs Black, had spent three months in psychiatric hospital before Irena returned to her at the age of three. The hospital provided good after-care and her social worker visited weekly, which Irena's mother found helpful because:

I could talk to her about how I felt.

Nonetheless, Mrs Black commented:

It took a long time for Irena to trust me again... I think she needed me to prove that I loved her.

Irena was fortunate to have been able to continue at the nursery school she had attended before entering care until she started school; she saw the social worker weekly for the first six months and her school was helpful. In addition, a befriender was arranged for her mother, who also received disability benefit so that her income increased. Mrs Black could go back to the psychiatric hospital whenever she wanted to in order to talk to the staff and she had support from her parents and friends. She commented:

The quality of help and support you get is very high in Greentown ... The social worker is there if I need anything and the help is excellent.

Residential assessment and treatment, including mother and baby placements

Another five of the successful returns were preceded by residential assessment and assistance. For example, Kim returned to live with her parents Mr and Mrs Guest in the community, after the whole family had spent many months in an intensive therapeutic residential family treatment centre. Mrs Guest said that the treatment was very painful and felt 'like hell' but helped her a lot. The parents also had couple therapy and support from other patients. When the family returned to live in the community (which was considered to be the return), Mrs Guest attended therapy twice a week, which she saw as essential for the success of the return. Clearly the intensive treatment in this particularly challenging case had made a major contribution to the child's safe and successful return to her parents.

It was also noticeable that a number of successful returns occurred after mother and baby foster placements. This may have been because of the assessment and help provided to mothers in this situation during and after the placement and because some of the mothers did have the capacity to parent well but had been very young or had other difficulties when their babies were born. In some of these cases, support was provided for a considerable length of time after the mothers and their babies settled into the community. For example, Jenna and her mother were in a mother and baby foster placement because the mother was very young and had learning difficulties. When Jenna was six months old, she and her mother went to live in a flat, where the social worker and a family support worker visited twice weekly. Jenna attended day nursery and a psychologist gave advice to her mother. Everything was going well at the two-year follow-up.

Return to the other parent who did not have difficulties

Two successful returns occurred when children had been removed from one parent who had difficulties and returned to the other parent who did not. Leo, for example, had been unable to live with his mentally ill mother but was placed with his father at the age of three, after almost two years in care. Family support workers assisted the father before and after Leo's return and his social worker provided towels, curtains and other material assistance before Leo went home. His father managed with daily support from his parents, which enabled him to maintain his job.

Return after an abusing parent had left the household

Returns also went well when an abusing parent left the family and the caring parent did not resume their relationship with them. Nick, for example, who had been physically abused by his father, returned to his mother and her new partner at the age of eight months with support from the partner's parents. His mother commented that it was much easier living with her partner, who got on well with Nick, than it had been being with Nick's father, who was a drug addict.

Adolescent returns which were well supported and where the parents coped better

Reunification was often less straightforward when it concerned young people with behavioural and emotional difficulties. Nonetheless, in four of the interview cases these returns were well supported and the parents were better able to cope. Chris, for example, was a young person who had been looked after because of his difficult and aggressive behaviour. His first return home had not worked out but, after another nine months in care, his second return was successful, partly it appeared because of a range of supports for the placement and partly because he had learned to control his temper. Regular respite care was provided to support the return for a year and a psychiatrist put Chris on Ritalin, which was effective. Chris had been involved in anger management sessions while in care and had found ways to control his aggression. The school was very supportive to his mother and a school counsellor saw Chris. His social worker also took Chris out for chats, was 'brilliant' and also gave his mother back-up. His mother said of the social worker:

> He was there for me. I could phone if I had any problems . . . I wasn't on my own. They would help . . . They were like family in the end.

Chris could also talk to his mother's new partner. He valued the respite care and was enthusiastic about his Year Head, who was his mentor and confidante and gave him a great deal of support. Chris explained:

> I've learned self-control . . . Care made me mature more quickly . . . I love being at home now . . . I'd hate to go back into foster care.

Sophie's return was made possible because of a favourable change in the family composition and the provision of support. She was a child with severe emotional and behavioural difficulties, for whom a therapeutic placement had been recommended but not agreed. She had been in care between the ages of four and 10 and returned home after her mother removed her from her children's home where she had been abused by another child. There were clearly a number of reasons, such as her long period in care at a young age and the lack of preparation for return, which might have suggested that her return would not work. Initially, there were many arguments with her mother, as well as lying and truanting from school. However, Sophie formed a good bond with her mother's new husband who could exert some control over her and she had monthly respite care rising to fortnightly. The social worker visited monthly and although the mother would have preferred more frequent visits, she reported that she was managing Sophie 'a lot better than before' and was firmer in her discipline.

Sophie herself reported that she was 'surprised that it has worked out' and 'thankful'. She said that she now got on better with her mother than before and had a good relationship with her stepfather. She had learned to go to her room when she was upset. She had remained in the same supportive school and she saw the social worker every three months, which she found helpful, although she did not confide in her. Thus, it appears that the presence of her stepfather and the intensive support provided for this reunification helped to make it work.

Adolescent return after intensive treatment and follow-up support

In one other case, the return appeared to be successful because of the intensive therapy a young person had received while in a secure unit and the follow-up support after he returned home. As we have seen, Phil had received help from a child psychiatrist and psychologist, as well as participating in family therapy sessions. Staff from the unit continued to work with Phil, his mother and his stepfather after he left, providing them with 'a network of people you could relate to' and who were at the end of a telephone if the need arose. In addition, Phil was fortunate to have a home tutor who helped to get him into college and provided Phil's mother with support at meetings. The social worker saw Phil and his parents separately every fortnight. Phil 'got on brilliantly with her' and his mother and stepfather liked her too. She had helped to give his mother confidence that she would be able to manage Phil. Moreover, the unit had prepared her for what to expect and she had learned how to think out alternative strategies to manage him after attending two parenting skills programmes. His mother reported that, when Phil returned home this time, he had changed for the better:

Although he still was angry and frustrated, he'd learned other ways to deal with it . . . he was a lot more calmer about things than what he was before.

Parents' views of unsuccessful returns

The interviews with parents suggested a number of reasons why returns did not work out, some of which are the flipside of the reasons for the successful reunifications.

Return to an unchanged situation

One major group of unsuccessful returns (seven cases or 37% of the failed returns) were those where children returned to the same situation that had precipitated the need for them to enter care, without any improvements in the original problems.

Parent–child relationship difficulties

In two of the three cases where there were particularly severe parent–child relationship difficulties, the returns were made on the recommendation of the court and against the wishes of the children's services department.

For example, adoption was planned for Jack and his younger sister but during care proceedings the children's guardian, psychiatrist and psychologist recommended return to their mother. Considerable support was provided for the return, including play therapy for Jack who had just started school, a specialist class at school, a family support worker twice a week, behavioural therapy, respite care and a parenting course for his mother. However, Jack's mother admitted 'My life was probably too chaotic to manage.' She was overwhelmed by Jack's behaviour, which escalated in severity until the return broke down. Jack then had a number of placements in care and another failed return and was only contained later in an out-of-county residential placement.

Alcohol problems

Another example of a return to parents whose problems were unchanged was the Malouf family, where the mother had a serious alcohol problem but had received no treatment. Her older son, Akram, had had an

143

extremely unsettled and unstable childhood with exposure to parental violence, physical abuse, drugs and alcohol misuse by his mother and her many partners, and many admissions to care. He returned yet again to his mother at the age of 14 in an unplanned move because of a placement disruption. The social worker visited fortnightly to monitor the situation but had not provided support. Mrs Malouf's serious alcohol problem continued and Akram returned to care after five months, feeling suicidal.

The only mention of treatment in this case was that, after being on a waiting list for a year, a 'drink social worker' had visited briefly but had then left. Mrs Malouf commented on the lack of assistance or treatment:

> They sit and wait, don't they? And it's like 'Oh, well you've cracked up again. We're taking them [the children] now.' They just sit and wait, watch you do it. They don't support you.

In another such case, Tracey was aged seven when she returned to her mother, who misused alcohol and had mental health problems. She missed her foster carers but did not confide in her social worker, on her mother's advice. Her mother, in turn, did not tell the social worker how difficult she found Tracey's behaviour. In the interview, she said, 'Last few weeks have been fine but apart from that it's been hell'. Tracey was injured in a violent argument between her mother and stepfather and was physically abused by her mother. Whilst this return was continuing at follow-up, it appeared detrimental for Tracey, who made it clear in interview that she did not feel close to her mother.

It was noticeable how often parents had received no treatment for their alcohol problems before their children were returned to them and how there would often then be a series of unsuccessful returns, with the children oscillating back and forth between care and their parents.

Mental health problems

Similarly, a few parents who had mental health problems (with no accompanying substance misuse difficulties) were unable to provide a satisfactory standard of care for their children. Returns to these parents seemed, on balance, not to be in the children's best interests, although the judgement of whether they were or were not the least worst option for the children had not always been easy to make. For example, Graham's mother, Mrs Selby, had a long history of physical and mental health problems and unpredictable behaviour. At the age of 10, Graham entered care for the third time at his mother's request but was rapidly removed by his mother and returned home. A worker from CAMHS who assisted Mrs Selby expressed concern that she was emotionally abusing her son and using him to gain services for herself. Graham was supported by a mentor by means of respite care, which he enjoyed, and by his school where, in spite of their help, he was unhappy. In interview, Mrs Selby was uniformly negative about Graham and said that both she and Graham would have preferred it if Graham had been in care. In view of Graham's distress about living at home, we concluded that the return was not successful.

Return after parental improvement but where problems of domestic violence re-emerge

Another group of unsuccessful returns (three cases) were those where there had been some improvements at home, but serious difficulties emerged or re-emerged later, leading to a poor-quality return or to breakdown. These difficulties often involved domestic violence.

In one example, where the parents were misusing drugs and alcohol, their baby was returned to them at the age of four months. The family centre, health visitor and social worker were involved and the mother attended parenting classes and a mother and baby group. She also received some support from her parents. No help was offered to the father or to either parent in relation to their substance misuse or their relationship difficulties. After the father was very violent to the mother and the police were called out twice in one day, the baby was removed and placed permanently with relatives.

Return where an abusing parent rejoined the household

Returns could also fail if a parent or partner who was considered to put the children at risk returned to the family. For example, Luke and Sam were removed on emergency protection orders after Sam, who was still a baby, was found to have fractures. The father was imprisoned. The mother had to attend a family centre several times a week to improve her parenting skills. She said:

Social services had you on the run all the time.

The children were returned to their mother on care orders and with a support package in place. However, after the father was released from prison, it was discovered that the parents were meeting in secret and the father was seeing the children. A core assessment then concluded that the children should be placed for adoption.

Adolescent returns to an unchanged situation

Eight of the 19 unsuccessful returns (42%) concerned adolescents and pre-adolescents where neither the young people nor their parents had made any substantial changes. All too often neither the parents nor the young people had received any help or specific interventions to bring about change. It was generally not enough to hope that simply being looked after would lead to improvements in the young people's behaviour. Some of these young people, as we have seen, returned to their families precipitately either because the placements were no longer willing to tolerate their behaviour or because their parents considered them to be at risk from others in the placement.

Insufficient intervention prior to return

Robbie, for example, had been beyond the control of his father and was returned to his mother and her partner at the age of 12 after more than a year in care because he wanted to return. However, once there his behaviour deteriorated; he was shoplifting, lighting fires and truanting from school and the return only lasted three months. A psychiatrist had suggested that Robbie needed a specialist residential unit but neither the education or children's services department had agreed to pay for it.

Adolescent returns where prior intervention had led to insufficient change

Sometimes, although intervention had been provided, too little change had occurred before a child returned home. For example, Tina was in care because of her frequent suicide threats. The local CAMHS team were involved and gave advice leading to Tina's return home at the age of 13 after five months in foster care. The team remained involved with Tina and her mother, seeing Tina fortnightly. Nonetheless, the mother felt that no one had got to grips with Tina's difficulties:

Even now, I wish that somebody would listen to me and think: 'Hang on. There's something wrong'. . . Nobody was actually helping us.

Tina's mother considered in retrospect that Tina had come home too early. Tina herself had been scared when she returned that it would be as before. She found that her mother:

. . . was not there [for me] in the way that I wanted her to be.

She missed the foster carers, where she had felt nurtured, and did not get on with her mother's partner, who drank heavily and was violent to her. Tina truanted from school where she was not coping with the work, struggled with depression and took further overdoses. The return broke down after 11 months.

Returns which were poorly supported

In addition to the lack of interventions to bring about change for children and parents, many of the unsuccessful returns were poorly supported. Ross, for example, had a combination of learning and behavioural difficulties from an early age. He was considered to have ADHD, oppositional defiance disorder and was on Ritalin. He was accommodated at the age of seven because of his aggression. He had four placements in care, but in the last one he was injured so that his mother, Mrs Shaw, took him home. Mrs Shaw found his behaviour volatile and worse than before he had gone into care and he, in turn, blamed his mother for his experiences in care. Mrs Shaw said:

We were walking on eggshells waiting for Ross to explode.

Ross was on the waiting list for respite care for 18 months. Mrs Shaw told us that she rang the emergency duty team 40 times for advice and that Ross ignored the social worker on his monthly visits. Nonetheless, Ross did see a psychiatrist at CAMHS for some time. However, he was excluded from school and started to offend. The return broke down after Ross assaulted his mother but he made progress in a subsequent specialist foster placement, with additional support from a sessional worker. Mrs Shaw compared the additional help provided to the foster carers with the lack of support for the return to her:

> He's getting enough sessional workers and this and that . . . when Ross was at home we couldn't even get somebody to come and give respite for an hour a month. [Now] Ross gets four hours respite three times a week.

Premature case closure

A few cases were closed prematurely. For example, Alex had ADHD, was aggressive to his siblings, and was accommodated when he was nearly 13 because his mother could not control him. He saw a psychologist for anger management sessions and attended a boys' group. He returned home after three months in care with various supports initially in place: the social worker visited weekly, which was seen as helpful; a Youth Centre provided day trips; and a psychiatrist saw Alex for his ADHD and provided family sessions. However, the case was closed after two months because of the improvement in Alex's behaviour. After eight months, Alex told children's services that his parents were hitting him regularly and that he did not want to be at home. He was stealing, showing difficult behaviour and assaulted a child in school. After an initial assessment, a youth offending team worker and an outreach worker became involved. In spite of this range of difficulties or because of the involvement of other professionals, the case was then closed again.

Returns *faute de mieux*

Some returns had a poor chance of success because they were made *faute de mieux* when agencies considered that there were few other options, although a return had little likelihood of success. For example, Hannah had been neglected and physically abused as a child and was accommodated with foster carers when she was aged 14. Her father then removed her from school and Hannah refused to return to her foster placement, so this was accepted as a *fait accompli*. Hannah revealed that it was 'really bad' at her father's, that she did not get on with her older brother, who always put her down, that she was drinking, using drugs and fighting with her father as well as at school. She had anger management sessions but the therapist 'was digging up the real roots of the past and I didn't like it . . . It brought back too many memories in one go' and so she stopped attending. In spite of the poor quality of this return, the case was closed and by a year later, the return had broken down. By this time, Hannah was unemployed and depressed and had tried to commit suicide a number of times.

The parent's views on what had been crucial and what other help was needed

In addition to considering the success or failure of the returns, we asked the parents what had helped and what other assistance might have made the returns work. The mother who had made good use of treatment for her drinking problem emphasised that:

> *People who are going to receive help have got to want it, otherwise there's no point in having it . . . You've just got to do it yourself.*

Indeed, her daughter Julie had had two previous unsuccessful returns because her mother had continued to drink heavily. It appeared that her mother became more motivated to tackle her difficulties later when she realised that she would lose her daughter if she did not. Being clear with parents about the consequences of their taking no action to improve is obviously an important part of the social work role in such cases. It is sometimes only when confronted with the reality of losing their children, that parents with serious problems, particularly those involving addiction, make attempts to change (see also Ward *et al*, 2010).

Parents had ideas about what additional help would have been beneficial. Leo's father thought that work with Leo's mother should have stopped sooner, in which case his son would have come to live with him earlier. He also said that it would have helped him if he could have talked to others who were in the same situation as he was. He had got to know another single father from work and found talking to him helpful. Three other parents said that they too would have liked to talk to other parents who were in the same situation (see also Farmer and Parker, 1991).

Mrs Kaur, whose daughter's return was not successful, had felt that children's services 'was out to get me' and that her worker was always bringing up 'every negative point that she could find'. She felt that her social worker had relied on her history without assessing her parenting ability afresh. She said that she had found the family centre workers more helpful and less threatening than her social worker, but had still wanted more one-to-one work, especially to provide emotional support and to build up her confidence as a parent. (She had later discovered an organisation for the partners of drug users, which may have been the kind of targeted resource she most needed.) Indeed, a number of the mothers felt that it would also have helped if their social workers had had more confidence in them as parents. As one said:

One minute they trust me and the next they're saying they don't.

Josie's mother had wanted children's services to listen to her more. Indeed, parents quite often said that their social workers had not listened to them and this was true even when the returns had been successful. As we have seen, four mothers considered that they had needed help with their children's behaviour from a much earlier age. They felt that no one had listened to their concerns. One said:

I think if we'd been given support and help a lot earlier it might have been different.

Seven parents said that they would have found it useful if they had had more support for themselves, including counselling, and they had wanted their worries to be taken on board, three had wanted more social work visits, and five parents wished that they had had help with behaviour management.

Ten of the parents (evenly divided between those with successful and unsuccessful returns) considered that respite care would have been helpful, one parent would have liked help with child sitting and another a place in a nursery school.

Quite a number of parents felt that the workers considered the children's needs to the exclusion of those of their parents and many of the parents of adolescents, as we have seen, wanted social workers and other professionals who would challenge their children about their poor behaviour and not reward difficult behaviour with meals out or similar activities. Six parents had also wanted psychiatric help, anger management, a mentor or simply someone who could talk to their children, whilst three had wanted a family support worker or activity groups for their children.

One father too had wanted help after he had physically abused his son; two sets of parents said that the father had needed help because of his violence to the mother and two others had wanted assistance with their drugs and alcohol misuse problems.

Now that the parents' views of the returns and services have been explored, we look at the children's experiences of reunification.

Children's views of relationships with their parents and of the returns

Of the 19 young people interviewed, just under half (9) had had a successful return. When asked about their main feeling about being at home, 11 of them had felt fairly happy, although five expressed much more negative feelings. However, in addition, nine young people (just under half) said that they also felt sad, upset, jealous, confused or angry. Seven of the children (a third) missed their foster carers, children's homes and the routines, security and activities they had enjoyed there, whilst 12 (two-thirds) young people found things difficult at home.

We asked the young people who they had felt most and least close to during the study return. Ten of the children said that they had been (or were) closest to their mothers, four to their fathers (or their mother's partners) and two to their siblings, whilst three did not feel close to anyone in the family. During these returns only a third of the children felt that their parents were really there for them and interested in them.

Of the young people whose returns were still continuing at the time of the interview, seven reported that they had a good, three a fair and two a poor relationship with their mothers. Relationships with fathers or the mother's partner were good in six out of the seven relevant cases.

Lindy, for example, was accommodated for just two months before her return. She described feeling like 'the black sheep in the family' with her parents favouring her sister and said that whilst she had a good relationship with her father, she had a difficult relationship with her mother, seeing it as 'both our fault – mother and I'. Lindy felt happy to be home but scared that 'I wouldn't get on with my mother again'. She explained:

Mum and I aggravate each other although we love each other . . .
I don't get on with them when I live at home but I miss them when
we're separated.

The children's views of their relationships with family members, friends and professionals during the returns

During the interviews, we asked children to fill in an ecomap. The child was in the centre and they wrote the names of other people in their lives at that time, placing those who were closest or most important in the inner circles and others in the outer circles. We did this to help to explore children's relationships and particularly how they saw those with their parents and other family members and friends.

Fifteen of the 19 children placed their mothers in the inner circle showing that they felt close to them whilst the other four placed their mothers in the second circle, further away from them. Most children put the names of other family members such as fathers, stepfathers, siblings and sometimes other relatives and a best friend in the inner circle, whilst three put the names of a teacher or head teacher, one a foster carer and one her mentor this close to them. One young man who had a successful return nonetheless placed noone in the inner circle on his eco-map.

In the second circle, which indicated fairly close relationships, children often put other relatives and friends, two named teachers, three foster carers, one her key worker in a residential unit and another a community support worker whom she was seeing weekly. In the outer circle much further away, three children placed their fathers, two their social workers, two their teachers or workers from school and one his last foster carer.

The children's views of their difficulties during the returns

The young people described a range of difficulties after they went home. Two had got on particularly poorly with their mothers' partners. For example, Tina was afraid of her mother's violent partner who drank and hit her and on one occasion pinned her to the floor. She was angry with her mother for not standing up for her in relation to him:

My mother picks dickheads for partners.

One girl stopped attending school after her brother died from a drugs overdose. In another case, a young man was suspended from his school:

I went downhill big time . . . All the anger and hurt inside of me . . . I was just letting it out . . . Every day of my life I've had people dragging me down and putting me down. I've always had people hitting me every day, talking to me like I'm crap, saying I should be dead.

Three young people became depressed, including the two who were no longer attending school, who also became isolated. One of them made a number of suicide attempts and a young woman became severely depressed and saw a psychiatrist fortnightly. She contrasted the difficult experiences she had had with her birth family with foster care, which she missed and where she had felt loved and the centre of attention.

Two children described feeling abandoned and lonely. A third young person was aged only 16 when she became pregnant and her parents initially refused to help, which left her feeling lost. A fourth young man felt abandoned when he returned to a mother who did not relate to him. His mother had taken him home against the advice of children's services and he ran away after only one day when his mother was drunk:

I had just had enough . . . I just couldn't hack being there . . . I just felt abandoned really and angry.

Since then he had remained in care, having had six placements by follow-up.

153

Six young people described their own continuing behaviour difficulties, which had contributed to return breakdown, including two who were aggressive and violent to parents or siblings and two who became involved in anti-social peer groups. For example, one said:

My behaviour went downhill. I just lost the plot. I was beating up my parents and running off. I don't know why. It was my own fault. I kept saying I wanted to return to care.

Two other children talked about relationship problems with their parents. Two others were either physically abused or much neglected during the return. Three young people drank excessively, one of whom ended up in prison. Two of the three, as well as drinking and smoking cannabis, were living with parents who themselves misused drugs (Lynskey *et al*, 1994).

Two girls had contrasting difficulties because of their mothers' mental illness. One girl of 10 was home with her mother only for a month before her mother was re-hospitalised because of her mental health problems.

It upset me a little bit but I knew it was best for her.

She returned to her original foster carers, where she stayed, and was happy and able to benefit from outdoor sports, such as horse riding. She saw her social worker regularly.

In contrast, Graham who was also aged 10 when returned home was, as we have seen, very unhappy living with his mentally ill mother. He had worried about returning to his mother because of her mental health problems and negativity to him. He had frequent arguments with his mother and did not feel close to her:

I didn't think, like, that she cared, like, or anything.

He bottled up his difficulties and took it out at school, where he got into fights and was a loner. He also developed an eating disorder and was not sleeping and particularly disliked the six-week holidays when he could not escape to school, which he saw as:

A nightmare . . . I like being out of the house.

Graham felt jealous that 'all my friends have really good home lives and stuff' and that he had to take on much more responsibility than they did, including doing the washing and ironing. When asked about the worst things about being at home, Graham said:

Having to live with my mum.

In addition, Tracey, who had returned to her mother who misused alcohol and neglected her, had also, as we have seen, not wanted to return:

I wanted to stay in care . . . I did enjoy it more [in care] than staying here.

The children's understanding of why their returns had succeeded

The nine children whose returns had gone well gave a variety of reasons for their success.

Changes in the children

Seven said that they themselves had changed or matured and were now behaving better. For example, Alice was 11 when she returned to her mother, who had finally stopped drinking. She thought this return had worked better than the previous ones:

Probably because I'm older, like, I understand better.

Chris was clear that he had changed, partly as a result of intensive help from a variety of sources whilst he was in care. Sophie similarly had learned to go to her room when she was upset and Sheila said that she no longer argued:

I walk away because I'm older.

Carrie said that her time in care had made her more independent and helped her to change her behaviour:

I mean, going there's made me realise how I made my mum feel. You've got to work at it.

155

Jamie, who had returned at the age of 15 from more than two years in an independent residential unit, had attended an anger management course there, but his behaviour had continued to be very violent. However, his return was very well supported. Jamie was generally better behaved and had fewer rows with his mother, even though he had 'an up and down relationship' with her but he missed the activities from his placement. His mother thought that the return had worked partly because she was on her own and had no partner, whilst he saw the return as working out 'because it had to', which seemed to mean that he knew he had to behave better as the alternative would have been placement in a secure unit.

Changes in the parents

Two returns had clearly worked because mothers had overcome their alcohol problems. For example, as we have seen, Julie had returned to her mother because her social worker thought she was mature enough and her mother had stopped drinking, although Julie herself was worried that this might not last. The return worked well, in Julie's words, because:

> Mum's got better. I prefer it here more than anywhere else . . . I think I'm more understanding . . . I respect what my mum does for me.

Changes in the parent–child relationship

Four returns were assisted by improvements in the parent–child relationships or the fact that young people made good relationships with the parent's partner. Sophie and Chris, for example, formed good relationships with their mothers' partners and got on better with their mothers. Two other children, who had poor relationships with their mothers, formed a good bond with their stepfathers.

Other relationships

Three of the young people made good relationships with a boyfriend or girlfriend, which helped them to become more stable. Two were buoyed up by the prospects of developing a career or were awaiting places at a college for further training.

As we have seen, in some cases these improvements were developed or sustained with help from a variety of services from professionals or the maintenance of links with former foster carers.

The children's views of what other help they had needed

We asked the young people if there had been anything else that would have made being at home easier. Ten children did not think so. However, a few would have welcomed help from school or social work assistance for themselves, their families or to work on their relationships with their parents.

Indeed, two young women had specifically wanted help with communication with their mothers and work on the mother–daughter relationship. One said:

> *Just help with the family really. 'Cos they all turned their back on me. Just didn't want to know.*

Another young woman had wanted someone to hear her side of the story and not just listen to her mother; two others had wanted not only to be listened to but also 'someone to care'. Another young person would have liked his social worker to take him out more often, telephone more and ask him how he felt.

Two young people wished that they had had the chance to talk to other young people from the care system who had shared their experiences. For example, Mandy found the mentor who worked with her "really good" and quite liked her social worker. However, she said:

> *It would have been easier if I could've talked to someone who's been in and out of care like me. I couldn't talk to the social worker – I thought they were 'really high up'.*

Similarly, Hannah, who had been unable to use sessions with a therapist because they were too painful, said that instead:

> *I wanted someone to listen and to care, someone who'd been through the care system like me.*

Two other young people wanted to be in care and not at home and a few children, as we have seen, had wanted more preparation and time before returning.

Now that the children's views have been examined, we consider the social workers' perspectives on the returns. Of the 22 social workers whom we interviewed, half (10) spoke of successful returns and half (12) of those that were unsuccessful.

The social workers' views of the successful returns

Social workers were asked what they thought were the critical factors that had sustained the returns in the 10 successful cases. They pointed to the provision of respite care (in one case provided by a relative) as a crucial factor, such that some returns would not have survived without it. In other cases, the critical factor that sustained the return was seen as intensive specialist help for both the parents and the child (from residential centres for families or children) or the provision of supportive mother and baby placements, which had assisted the mothers to be ready to move with their babies into the community. In two cases there had been a combination of the parents being better able to cope and improvements in their children's behaviour.

The interviews with the parents and children had suggested that another crucial factor for a few young people was their own determination to make the return work, combined with increased maturity. In this context, it is worth noting that some workers were particularly committed to making returns work and to providing the resources to make this possible.

The social workers' views of the unsuccessful returns

Seven social workers thought that the return had been unsuccessful because the problems in the family had not been adequately addressed, and one because the family had been given insufficient support to sustain the child's return. In two cases, the failure of the returns was seen as linked to the fact that they were initiated by the parents and were unplanned. In one case, new problems had arisen as the child became involved in criminal activity whilst at home, resulting in court proceedings. In the view of the social worker, this child returned home *only* because there was no suitable placement available for him and with no one expecting the return home to last for any length of time.

The social workers' views of the impact of return breakdown on the children and parents

Seventeen social workers were able to rate the return as a whole in terms of its effect on the child. Ten thought that the return had been detrimental for the children because of their experiences at home and because of the impact of the breakdown on them. For example, one worker thought that return had been 'enormously negative and devastating' for the child. Another social worker said of the child:

> *Emotionally she was completely gutted that her mother couldn't handle her.*

For some children the return breakdown had been negative for the children and their parents, because there had been a complete breakdown in the relationship between the children and parents and their parents had refused to continue to care.

However, in contrast, the impact of the return ending was described as positive for three children. One young girl left her mother, who was having problems with domestic violence and drugs misuse, and went to live with her father. For the other two children, the ending of the return home was described as a relief: one child, because she had left the mother who drank heavily and emotionally and physically abused her and the other child, because he had left his parents by running back to his foster carers.

Now that the parents', children's and social workers' accounts of what had helped to make the returns succeed or fail have been given, we turn to examine what the statistical analyses showed were the key factors associated with return outcomes.

Summary

The parents' views of the returns

- Of the returns to the 34 parents we interviewed, 15 had been successful at the two-year follow-up stage and 19 had not. The interviews with parents revealed that there were a range of situations in which reunification was successful.

- Returns were successful when there had been an improvement in parental difficulties either because of treatment for the parents or the help provided to them in residential centres and mother and baby placements. Other returns had succeeded because an abusing parent had left the family or the child had returned to the other parent who did not have difficulties. The adolescent returns had succeeded either as a result of very intensive treatment and follow-up support or when there had been an improvement in the parents' capacity to cope, which had been sustained by good support during the return.

- One major group of unsuccessful returns were those where children returned to the same situation that had precipitated the need for them to be looked after, without any improvements in the original problems.

- Another group of unsuccessful returns were those where there had been some improvements, but serious domestic violence emerged or re-emerged later, leading to a poor-quality return or breakdown. Returns could also fail if a parent or partner who was considered to put the children at risk returned to the family.

- Eight of the unsuccessful returns concerned adolescents and pre-adolescents where neither the young people nor their parents had made any substantial changes. In others there had been some but insufficient change. Many of the unsuccessful returns were poorly supported.

- A few other unsuccessful cases were closed prematurely before problems had resolved and with insufficient services in place. Some returns had had little likelihood of success because they were made *faute de mieux* when agencies considered that there were few other options.

- The parents described a range of services that they would have found useful, including treatment for their alcohol or drugs misuse problems, respite care and help with behaviour management.

The children's views of the returns

- The young people described the kinds of difficulties they faced after they went home. Three had been depressed and four described feeling lonely and abandoned.
- The children suggested a range of reasons why their returns had succeeded (nine successful returns). Seven said that they had changed or matured and were now behaving better. Other returns were assisted by improvements in the parent–child relationship, the fact that young people made good relationships with the parent's partner or with a boyfriend or girlfriend or because a parent had overcome their alcohol problems. In some cases, these improvements were developed or sustained with help from a variety of services, including from former foster carers.

The social workers' views of the returns

- The social workers considered that the critical factors in sustaining the successful returns were the provision of respite care, specialist help for both the parents and the child or the provision of supportive mother and baby placements which had enabled the mothers to be ready to move with their babies into the community.
- The social workers thought that the reasons for the 11 return breakdowns in the social worker interview sub-sample were because the problems in the family had not been adequately addressed or more rarely because the family had been given insufficient support to sustain the child's return.
- Social workers saw the study return as positive for six of the children but as detrimental for another 10.

10 The stability and quality of the children's returns

This chapter describes the outcome of the returns in terms of their stability, that is, whether they were continuing or not by the end of the two-year follow-up period. The factors associated with return stability are highlighted and logistic regression analyses are used to show which of these factors best predict return stability. Since the quality of the continuing returns varied considerably, we then consider the factors that were associated with good-quality returns. The reasons for return disruption are examined in Chapter 11.

The stability of the returns for the full sample of children

By the end of the two-year follow-up period, of the 180 returns, almost half (47%) had ended. (This compares with a return disruption rate of 52% of accommodated children followed up for two years in Packman and Hall's (1998) study and 37% in Sinclair *et al*'s (2005) three-year follow-up of a cross-sectional sample of children returned home from foster care.) Forty-six per cent of the returns (83) were continuing and for seven per cent the outcome was not known, for example, because their cases had been transferred to another authority (see Figure 10.1)

The quality of the returns for the full sample of children

As we have seen, researcher ratings of the quality of the returns were made as follows:

> *Good quality* – Returns that were positive or adequate for the child. This category included cases where there were some difficulties or adverse incidents but, on the whole, circumstances for the child were adequate or good.

Figure 10.1
Return stability at the end of the follow-up period

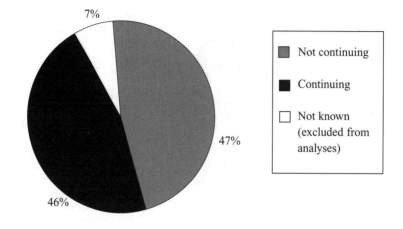

Borderline – Returns that included circumstances or incidents that were likely to be harmful for the child *or* where the parents were having difficulties managing the child, but where we did not consider that the return should have ended, either because the difficulties were not sufficiently serious or because, on balance, care would not have been a better option for the child.

Poor quality – Returns that were unacceptably harmful for the child and/or significantly limited his/her life chances, such that either they had ended or, in our opinion, should have been ended or where the parent was totally unable to cope with or contain the child's behaviour.

Of the 180 returns, over a quarter (28%) were considered to be of good quality, an eighth (14%) were borderline and half (49%) were rated as of poor quality (see Figure 10.2). (For 16 returns there was insufficient information to make these ratings or reunification had been temporary.)

Figure 10.2
Return quality at the end of the follow-up period

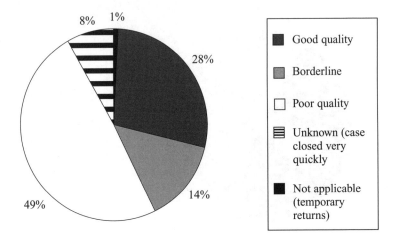

Return stability and quality for the full sample

Almost all (94%) of the 84 returns that had ended had been of poor quality. Of the 83 continuing returns, three-fifths (59%) were rated as of good quality, a quarter as borderline and an eighth as of poor quality (see Table 10.1).

Therefore, of the full 180 returns, at the end of the follow-up period the largest proportion (44%) had ended having been of poor quality (see

Table 10.1
Return stability by return quality

| Return quality | Return stability (at 2-year follow-up) | | | |
	Continuing (n = 83)	Ended (n = 84)	Not known (n = 13)	Total
Good quality	49 (59%)	1 (1%)	–	50 (28%)
Borderline	20 (24%)	2 (2.5%)	3 (23%)	25 (14%)
Poor quality	10 (12%)	79 (94%)	–	89 (49%)
Not known	4 (5%)	2 (2.5%)	10 (77%)	16 (9%)
Total	**83 (100%)**	**84 (100%)**	**13 (100%)**	**180 (100%)**

Figure 10.3). Just over a quarter (27%) were continuing and of good quality. A tenth (11%) were borderline but continuing and a small proportion (6%) were of poor quality and, worryingly, also continuing.

Figure 10.3
Return quality and stability

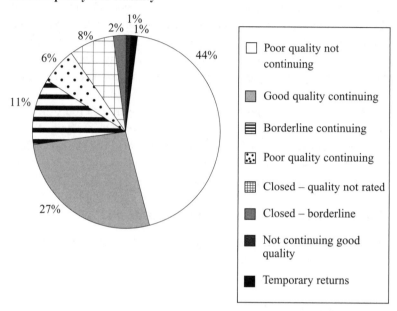

☐	Poor quality not continuing
▨	Good quality continuing
☰	Borderline continuing
⦂	Poor quality continuing
⊞	Closed – quality not rated
▦	Closed – borderline
■	Not continuing good quality
■	Temporary returns

Exploring the predictors of return stability: with one child per family (129 children)

The sample of 180 children from 141 families included 26 sibling groups. Twenty-four of those 26 sibling groups had the same outcome in terms of return stability at follow-up. Therefore, to limit any bias or duplication, only one child (the oldest) from a family was used for the analyses of stability and return quality which follow. In addition, for 12 of these 141 children, the outcome at the end of the two years was unknown. As a result, only 129 children were included in the analyses.

The characteristics and distribution by local authority of these 129 children were very similar to those in the full sample with, as would be expected, a slightly higher average age (8.45 as compared with 7.72 for the whole sample).

Since it is known that the care experiences of children differ by age (as do those of return [Farmer and Parker 1991]), the chi square analyses to explore the variables that predict reunification stability were conducted after splitting the sample into children who were under 11 and those aged 11 or over at the time of study return, as well as being undertaken for the whole group of 129 children. This age division was chosen as the age at which children start secondary school. Return stability was defined as a child still being with parent/s in the study return two years after reunification.

The results will be reported first for the younger age group, then for the over-11s and finally for the whole group of 129 children. When reporting significant associations, the results of Fisher's Exact Test (2-sided) or chi square results are given. For these first analyses, a p-value of 0.05 or less was considered significant.

Children aged 0–11 at return (69 children)

The 69 children who were aged 0 to just under 11 at the time of return to their parents had an average age of four-and-a-half with a range from babyhood to almost 11. The median age was five.

Demographic variables
None of the demographic variables were significantly associated with stability for this younger age group.

Pre-care history
Returns more often broke down when children had previously been physically abused or had experienced poor parenting, a category which included children being subject to aggressive or unresponsive parenting, lack of affection or inconsistent discipline.

Care period before return
A number of factors relating to the child's time in care before the study

return were significantly related to return stability for these younger children. Those who were only children, typically the first child of young parents, or who were adequately prepared for reunion had more stable returns. Not surprisingly, when all the key problems had been addressed, returns were more likely to be stable and this was also true when there was clear recording of the reasoning for a child's return (suggesting consistent practice and careful consideration of the appropriateness of reunion). In addition, when caregivers (usually foster carers) gave exceptional support for returns, reunification broke down less often.

The study return

When children returned to a different house from the one they had left, or a new partner, relative or sibling joined the family after children returned home, or another agency or professional (such as Barnardo's, the NSPCC or a health visitor) helped to supervise the return or adequate support was provided, the returns were more likely to be stable. In addition, as would be expected, if a child protection plan was discontinued or the case was closed subsequent to return, this was related to return stability.

On the other hand, when parents were ambivalent about the child's return, or the child was abused or neglected, or the original concerns arose again or the case was closed despite continuing concerns, the likelihood of return breakdown increased. In addition, if the parents were socially isolated or unable to cope or they showed anti-social behaviour, there were more return breakdowns.

Researcher ratings

The researchers rated each return after reading the entire case file. Two of these ratings were significantly related to return stability for children under 11 when they returned home. When children were receiving adequate parenting or they were close to their parent/s, their returns were more often stable.

Children aged 11-14 at return (60 children)

The older age group had an average (and median) age of almost 13 years at return.

Demographics

It was interesting to find that whether or not these older children experienced stable returns was significantly related to which local authority they lived in. Since this was not significant for the younger age group, this suggests that practice is more variable across authorities with older children.

Pre-care history

Where young people had siblings who had been maltreated prior to the return, there was a surprising finding. Those returns were more likely to be continuing at the end of the two-year follow-up period. This may be partly because these young people were significantly more likely to have been subject to a child protection plan prior to the return and to be returned home under care or supervision orders. As a result, they would have received oversight and, usually, assistance from children's services and other agencies.

Care period before return

In the very small number of cases where specific conditions were set for the young people about what needed to happen for them to return, the majority of their returns were stable. This could only occur in those situations where social workers were able to determine when the return took place and judged that young people might comply with such conditions and almost always specialist or social work help had also been provided. In addition, when there was not just a primary but also a second issue which facilitated return (such as improvements in the young person's behaviour or the parent–child relationship) there were fewer return breakdowns. Returns were also more stable when all the problems had been addressed prior to return, when children were returning from foster rather than residential care (which generally takes young people with higher levels of difficulties) and in the very small number of cases where young people were returned to assess whether or not their parents could care for them adequately, again suggesting close involvement by children's services.

The study return

Young people's returns were more stable if there had been a change in the parent or parent figures to whom they went. This could be the arrival or departure of a parent's partner or a move to the other parent (for example, if a child had lived with the mother but returned to a separated father). A positive change of this sort made a particular difference to the outcomes of the older group, possibly because of teenagers' conflicted relationships with single parents and their need for discipline. In addition, the imposition of specific conditions during return (such as about drugs or alcohol use, parenting standards or medical check-ups) was related to return stability, although conditions were not often used (15 cases only). Supervision by other agencies was again related to returns being stable, as was informal support and also high levels of such support from the wider family, friends or organisations like the church or Alcoholics Anonymous.

On the other hand, when more support was needed during the return, where there was serious conflict with a parent – often manifested in aggression or violence – there were more return breakdowns.

Researcher ratings

Young people who had had two or more failed returns were very much less likely to experience stable returns than others (Fisher's Exact Test $p = .0001$).

All children (129)

The factors that were significantly related to return stability for the whole group of 129 children were mostly the same as those already reported, although a few factors were significant only for the whole group of children.

Demographics

Importantly, the child's age at the time of the study return was significantly related to return stability (point bi-serial correlation $p<0.01$), with more of the younger children having stable returns. Return stability also varied significantly by local authority for the whole group of children.

Pre-care history

Returns were more likely to break down when there were concerns that the child had previously been physically abused, had experienced poor parenting or had previously been in care (and therefore previously returned home).

On the other hand, as we saw earlier, returns were more likely to be stable if the siblings of the study child had previously been abused or neglected.

Care period before return

Children who entered care with siblings had more stable returns as did those on court orders. Indeed, whilst 61 per cent of children on interim, care or supervision orders had stable returns, this was true for only 38 per cent of those who were accommodated, although, as we have seen, these children were generally older. When conditions had been set for the parents or for the children prior to return or when restrictions were attached to children's contact (which as we saw occurred most often for younger children), there were more stable returns (see also Sinclair *et al*, 2005), suggesting close involvement by children's services to protect children. Exceptional support by the caregivers for the returns, assessment prior to return, adequate preparation, pressure from parents for children to return to them (which implied motivation to care), clear recording of the reasons for reunification and all the key problems having been addressed were all related to returns being stable. In addition, if the primary or secondary reason for return was parental improvement of some sort (including changes in their housing or family composition or ability to cope), returns were more stable.

In contrast, if the timing of the return had been accelerated (for example, by a child absconding home) or there had been referrals but no service for children (suggesting unmet need for help) there were more return breakdowns.

The study return

A wide range of factors during the returns were significantly related to return stability for all the children. Changes in household membership by the time of the return of any sort (parents or parent figures, children or other adults) and more specifically the presence of a new father/figure or changes in the parents or their partners (arriving or leaving) as well as return to a different house were all related to return stability. Interestingly, later additions to families (parent/figures, relatives or children) were also related to stable returns, as was returning with siblings.

When parents admitted to having abused or neglected their child, returns were more stable. The imposition of conditions, other agency supervision and maintaining a clear picture of children's safety and progress were all related to return stability. When a voluntary organisation or other professional was supporting the returns (either alone or in conjunction with children's services) or when parents or children were receiving specialist help, their returns were more likely to last. Overall, when returns were adequately supported they were more likely to be stable. The provision of informal support too was important and high levels of informal support were related to returns more often lasting.

However, when parent/s had a history of ambivalence about the child, the case was closed after return despite concerns or more support was needed, returns more often broke down. No or frequent social work visits were related to return breakdown too, suggesting some oversight is important but that social work visits increase when returns were problematic. As might be expected, returns to parents whose parenting was poor or who were unable to cope more often broke down as did those where the original concerns arose again. When children had attachment-type difficulties (shown, for example, by separation anxiety which was inappropriate for age, emotional resistance, over-friendliness, clinging, frozen watchfulness or attachment disorders) or showed inappropriately sexualised behaviour, there was also an increased likelihood of return disruption.

Researcher ratings

Children who were close to at least one parent, who were receiving adequate parenting, who were not beyond control, who had not oscillated between home and care or who had no or only minor emotional and behavioural difficulties were more likely than others to experience stable returns.

The key factors that contributed to return stability

Having explored the association between each of the variables and the stability of reunification two years after placement, we then built statistical models to find out the most important of those factors when they were looked at together. These analyses were conducted using the whole group of children.

As most of the factors being considered were categorical variables and as the outcome was binary (return stability/breakdown), logistic regression was used. Logistic regression enables the calculation of the odds that a child would continue in the return. The variables that were included in the logistic regression models had to fulfill the following criteria:

- The chi square/Fisher's Exact Test result was significant at less than $p<0.025$.
- There was no multicollinearity between the variables. When the variables were highly correlated, only one was retained.
- Variables with more than 25 per cent of missing values were excluded.

The purpose was to build statistical models including the variables that met these criteria in order to find out which child, family and local authority or practice variables contributed most to stable reunifications by time period (before and after return). Return stability, as we have seen, was defined as still being with parent/s two years after reunification.

Prior to return – local authority and practice factors that contributed to return stability

To understand more about which local authority and social work practices affected outcome during the period just before reunification, a binary logistic regression was carried out with the variables that met all the criteria set out in the previous section. The coefficients of the final multivariate model are given in Table 10.2.

As can be seen, adequate preparation of the child and parent/s before reunification and the child's local authority were found to be significant predictors of reunification stability.

When there had been adequate preparation, the children were seven

Table 10.2
Predictors of return stability: social work practice and local authority factors before return

	Coefficient *t* *B*	*Odds* *ratio* *[exp(B)]*	*95% CI for odds ratio*	
			Lower	*Upper*
Intercept	−3.325***			
Specific conditions for parents prior to return	.519	1.680	.609	4.632
Clear recording of reason for return by the social worker	.198	1.219	.403	3.685
Adequate preparation for return by the social work team	1.990***	7.316	2.330	22.969
Local authority				
LA C (reference category)				
LA A	2.366***	10.659	2.614	43.453
LA B	2.952***	19.137	3.232	113.317
LA D	2.629*	13.857	1.206	159.207
LA E	1.452*	4.272	1.047	17.426
LA F	3.351*	28.535	1.941	419.591

$R^2 = .31$ (Cox and Snell) .41 (Nagelkerke), Model $\chi^2(5) = 39.70$, p<.001, *p<.05, **p<.01, ***p<.001

times more likely to have stable returns. The children in the sample came from six different local authorities and local authority C was set as the reference category in this analysis, against which the others were compared. Children from all of the five other authorities had better chances of having stable returns compared to the children from local authority C. Children from local authorities E, A and D were respectively 4, 10 and 14 times more likely and from authority B, 19 times and authority F, 28 times more likely to have a stable return, compared to children from local authority C. However, the numbers in each authority were small and the confidence intervals are large, so these findings should be viewed only as indicative.

After return – local authority and practice factors that contributed to return stability

The variables relating to the period after reunion that were included in the logistic regression model and the results are given in Table 10.3.

Table 10.3
Predictors of return stability: social work practice and local authority factors after return

	Coefficient B	Odds ratio [exp(B)]	95% CI for odds ratio	
			Lower	Upper
Intercept	–2.788***			
Legal status upon return	.319	1.375	.468	4.045
Specific conditions imposed during return	–.064	.938	.312	2.825
Other agency supervision	1.382**	3.984	1.410	11.256
Adequate support during return	1.213*	3.365	1.284	8.816
Local authority				
LA C (reference category)				
LA A	1.170	3.221	.899	11.537
LA B	1.655	5.232	1.103	24.816
LA D	2.607	13.556	.842	218.324
LA E	.582	1.790	.499	6.416
LA F	2.603	13.508	.871	209.384

$R^2 = .27$ (Cox and Snell) .37 (Nagelkerke), Model $\chi^2(5) = 37.03$, p<.001, *p<.05, **p<.01, ***p<.001

The results of this logistic regression indicate that, after reunification, the supervision of the children and their families jointly/solely by another agency (for example, another organisation or professional) and adequate support during return were both significant predictors of reunification stability. When there was supervision during return by another agency, the returns were four times more likely to be stable than when there was no other agency supervision. In addition, the returns which were adequately supported were three times more likely to be stable than those that were not well supported.

Prior to return – family factors that contribute to return stability

We continued the analysis by considering family factors prior to return, as can be seen in Table 10.4.

No previous physical abuse, exceptional support by the caregivers prior to return and pressure from parents for the child to be returned were all significant predictors of stable returns. Where there had been no concerns about physical abuse when they were taken into care, children

Table 10.4
Predictors of return stability: family factors before return

	Coefficient B	Odds ratio [exp(B)]	95% CI for odds ratio Lower	Upper
Intercept	−1.612*			
No previous physical abuse concerns	1.150*	3.158	1.160	8.600
No previous abuse of siblings by the carers the child was returned to	−.878	.416	.141	1.222
Number of siblings in the household before the child was taken into care				
None (reference category)				
1–2	.036	1.036	.170	6.337
3–5	1.162	3.196	.445	22.963
Exceptional support by caregivers prior to return	1.913**	6.776	1.658	27.684
Pressure from parents for the child to be returned	1.260*	3.525	1.339	9.280

R^2 = .24 (Cox and Snell) .32 (Nagelkerke), Model $\chi^2(6)$ = 27.47, p<.001, *p<.05, **p<.01, ***p<.001

were three times more likely to have a stable return than those where there had been worries about this. Returns were nearly seven times more likely to be stable when there was exceptional support by the caregivers prior to return than when there was no such assistance. In addition, where there was pressure from the parents for their looked after child to be returned to them, returns were nearly four times as likely to be stable than when there was no such pressure.

After return – family factors that contribute to return stability

We then considered family factors after reunification (see Table 10.5).

Table 10.5
Predictors of return stability: family factors after return

	Coefficient B	Odds ratio [exp(B)]	95% CI for odds ratio	
			Lower	Upper
Intercept	−3.578*			
Change to household composition since the last time child was home	3.150*	23.343	1.988	274.152
Lack of parental ambivalence	.749	2.114	.717	6.232
Support to parents from relatives/friends/community	−.393	.675	.231	1.975
No concerns about poor parenting during return	1.629*	5.098	1.450	17.924
Original concerns are not flagged up during return	−.087	.917	.244	3.441

R^2 = .24 (Cox and Snell) .33 (Nagelkerke), Model $\chi2$ (5) = 22.77, p<.001, *p<.05, **p<.01, ***p<.001

Changes in the family since the child had lived there and no concerns about poor parenting after return were both significant predictors of return stability. Children who returned to a family where the composition had changed since the child was last at home were 23 times more likely to have a stable return than were children who returned to the same household. When there were no reports of poor parenting after return, the children were five times more likely to have a stable reunion than where this did not apply.

Child factors that contributed to return stability

Finally, the child factors related to return stability were considered. As there were not as many significant child variables, the variables were not analysed by period (before and after return).

The child not showing attachment-type difficulties and not having a history of moving in and out of care were both significant predictors of reunification stability. The latter factor was predominantly a feature of the older children, which may be why age at return did not emerge as significant in this analysis.

Table 10.6
Predictors of return stability: child factors

	Coefficient B	Odds ratio [exp(B)]	95% CI for odds ratio	
			Lower	Upper
Intercept	−2.846			
Age at index return	.013	1.013	.890	1.154
No attachment-type difficulties during return	1.278*	3.591	1.009	12.781
No conflict/hostility with parents/carers during return	.638	1.892	.474	7.557
Child beyond parental control	−1.318	.268	.067	1.067
Child does not have a history of moving in and out of care (2+ failed returns)	2.364***	10.637	2.742	41.259

R^2 = .26 (Cox and Snell) .35 (Nagelkerke), Model $\chi2$ (4) = 30.66, p<.001, *p<.05, **p<.01, ***p<.001

Where there were no reports of children having attachment-type difficulties after return, children were nearly four times more likely to have a stable return than where there were such difficulties. Children who did not have a history of oscillating in and out of care were nearly 11 times more likely to have stable returns than those who were oscillators.

Now that we have considered the factors which predicted return stability, we look at those which were related to the quality of the ongoing returns.

Exploring the factors associated with the quality of the returns which were continuing at follow-up (N = 58)

Fifty-eight of the 129 children from the 141 families were still at home at the two-year follow-up. However, the quality of these continuing returns was extremely variable. It was therefore important to explore which factors could explain whether the quality of these returns would be good or poor and we do this in what follows. The numbers were too small to split these analyses by age as was done for return stability, so the results that follow are based on all 58 children. In addition, the numbers were not large enough to conduct any logistic regressions.

As can be seen in Figure 10.4 below, 56 per cent of these continuing returns were of good quality, whilst 44 per cent were of borderline or in most cases poor quality. (The way in which the quality of the returns was rated was described at the beginning of the chapter.) We turn now to consider the factors that proved to be significantly related to the quality of these returns, where the poor-quality and borderline returns were combined.

Demographics

Younger age was significantly related to the quality of these continuing returns. Two-thirds of the under-11s experienced good-quality reunions as compared with only a third of those 11 or over at return. Children with a physical disability were also more likely than others to have good quality returns.

Figure 10.4
The quality of the continuing returns

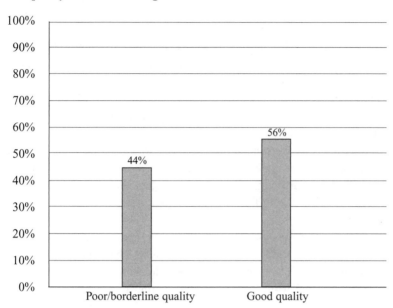

Care period before return

Returns of good quality were also related to the timing of reunion not having been accelerated, all the key problems having been addressed prior to return; or children entering care with siblings (which occurred more often with younger children).

The study return

In addition, reunions were of good quality when the parent/s did not have a history of ambivalence about the children, they were able to cope with them, there was no change of social worker, the parent/s cooperated with the social worker, conditions if set were enforced, the support provided was adequate, no more support was needed and there were no concerns about nursery or school attendance.

In contrast, returns were of poorer quality if the child was abused or neglected, or there were referrals about maltreatment or the original concerns arose again. Poor quality reunions were also more frequent when there was parental drugs or alcohol misuse, domestic violence or parental anti-social behaviour (such as damage to property or serious conflicts with neighbours), home life was unstable or unpredictable, there were serious financial problems or the child was poorly parented. (As we saw earlier, many of these difficulties were also associated with parental substance misuse.) Returns were also of poor quality when cases were closed despite concerns, cases that had been closed had to be re-opened later or referrals were made but services were not taken up or were unavailable. Poorer quality returns were also in evidence when children had behavioural difficulties or showed new difficult behaviour, they were in serious conflict with their parents or they were involved in high-risk relationships.

Overall, these analyses show that children under 11 more often than older children had stable returns and reunions which were of good quality. Those on care orders also had more stable returns. Consistent and purposeful social work both before and during reunification, including adequate preparation and setting of conditions, high levels of support for return by foster carers, adequate support overall, including specialist help during the returns, good parental motivation and the involvement of other agencies in monitoring and supporting returns were all related to returns lasting. Changes in the household to which children returned were associated with return stability, whereas children with a history of return breakdowns often had returns which failed yet again. Older children who had good informal support also had more stable returns. In addition, rates of return stability varied widely by local authority, especially for older children.

The continuing returns which were of good quality were marked again by purposeful social work where reunion was not rushed, parental difficulties had been addressed before the children went home and adequate support provided. In contrast, reunifications of poor quality more often arose when there was parental drugs or alcohol misuse or domestic violence, the original concerns arose again including abuse or neglect, or children showed renewed or new behavioural difficulties or were in conflict with their parents.

Now that we have considered the factors that were associated with return stability and continuing return quality, the next chapter shows why returns broke down and where the children went next.

Summary

- By the end of the two-year follow-up period, of the 180 returns, almost half (47%) had ended and most had been of poor quality (that is, unacceptably harmful for the children and/or significantly limiting of their life chances).
- Of the continuing returns, three-fifths (59%) were rated as of good quality but a third were rated as of borderline or poor quality.

Factors related to return stability for under- and over-11s

- 129 children were included in the analyses of factors that were related to return stability, after the exclusion of siblings and children whose outcomes were unknown. The analyses of return stability were conducted separately for children who were under 11 and those 11 or over at the time of study return, as well as being considered for the whole group of 129 children.
- *Pre-care.* The returns of older children whose siblings had been maltreated prior to the return were *more* likely to be continuing at follow-up, probably because of increased oversight. Return stability for the older age group also related to which local authority they lived in. Returns more often broke down for the younger children who had previously been physically abused or when they had experienced poor parenting.
- *The care period before return.* For the younger children, there were more stable returns when all the key problems had been addressed, there was clear recording of the reasoning for a child's return, there had been adequate preparation for reunion or caregivers (usually foster carers) gave exceptional support for returns. For the older children, returns were more stable where specific conditions were set before return, an issue such as improvements in the young person's behaviour

had facilitated return, all the problems had been addressed or children returned from foster rather than residential care.

- *During return*. For the younger children, the factors during reunion that related to return stability included returning to a different house, the arrival of a new family member, other agency supervision and the provision of adequate support. In contrast, when parents were ambivalent about the child's return, children were maltreated, the original concerns arose again or the parents were socially isolated, there were more return breakdowns. For the older children, the factors that related to return stability were fairly similar and also included having good informal support. On the other hand, when there was serious conflict with a parent, or young people had two or more failed returns, there were more return breakdowns.

Return stability for children of all ages

- A few other factors emerged as significant for the whole group of children. These included that there were more stable returns for the younger children, those on court orders or for children who entered care with siblings. There were also more stable returns when an assessment had been conducted prior to return, conditions had been set for the parents or restrictions were attached to children's contact.
- During return, other factors that were significantly related to return stability for children of all ages included the presence of a new father/figure and parental admissions of maltreatment. In addition, children who were close to at least one parent, were receiving adequate parenting, were not beyond control or who had no or few emotional and behavioural difficulties were more likely than others to experience stable returns. In contrast, when more support was needed, children had attachment-type difficulties or showed inappropriately sexualised behaviours, there was an increased likelihood of return disruption.

Logistic regression

- We then built statistical models to find out the *most important of these factors when they were looked at together* using logistic regression.

Prior to return, adequate preparation of the child and parent/s before going home, the child's local authority, no previous physical abuse, exceptional support by the caregivers, pressure from parents for the child to be returned and not having a history of moving in and out of care, were all significant predictors of stable returns.

- After reunion, return to a changed household, supervision of the children by another agency, adequate support, no concerns about poor parenting and the child not showing attachment-type difficulties were significant predictors of return stability.

Return quality

- Finally, we considered the factors that were significantly related to the quality of returns for those children still at home at follow-up. These included children being under 11 at return or having a physical disability, the timing of reunion not having been accelerated, all the key problems having been addressed and the children entering care with their siblings. In addition, reunions were of good quality when the parent/s did not have a history of ambivalence about the children, were co-operative, were able to cope, conditions if set were enforced, support was adequate and there were no concerns about nursery or school attendance.

- Poor quality reunions were more frequent when there was parental drugs or alcohol misuse, domestic violence, home life was unstable or unpredictable, there were serious financial problems or the child was poorly parented. Returns were also of poor quality when cases were closed despite concerns or when referrals were made but not taken up. Poorer quality returns were also in evidence when children had behavioural difficulties or showed new difficult behaviour, were in serious conflict with their parents or were involved in high-risk relationships.

11 The follow-up period

This chapter shows what happened next for the children whose returns broke down, including any later returns and where they ended up. The chapter finishes with children's and parents' accounts of their experiences of repeated unsuccessful reunification.

Reasons for returns ending

By the end of the two-year follow-up period, of the 180 returns, almost half (47%) had ended and all but five of these had been of poor quality. Three of these five had ended as a result of a planned move to care or a therapeutic family placement.

The primary and secondary reasons for the returns ending are shown in Table 11.1. As can be seen, parental problems were the dominant cause of return breakdown. Where previously abuse and neglect had been a major reason for many of the children becoming looked after, this was less often the reason for return disruption, with children's behaviour difficulties (or their decision to leave) assuming more prominence.

Table 11.1
Primary and secondary reasons for the returns ending

	Primary reason (n = 84)	Secondary reason (n = 84)	Total (n = 84)
Abuse or neglect	12%	10%	(22%)
Parent's difficulties or stress	57%	51%	(89%)
Child's behaviour	21%	19%	(39%)
Other	10%	8%	(15%)

NB. Figures in brackets are not column totals as cases have only been counted once where, for example, different forms of parental stress or illness were the primary and secondary reason for the return ending. No secondary reason in some cases.

The key issues affecting the parents' ability to care for their children were their mental health problems, drug or alcohol misuse and adult relationship issues including domestic violence and relationship breakdown. Sometimes parental care or discipline was inadequate, parents were unwilling to care for their children or the parent–child relationship had broken down.

Children's services (28%) or the court (5%) intervened to protect a third of the children. In many cases (43%) parents recognised their difficulties and took action to end the returns. In the remainder, the breakdown of the return was initiated either by the child (16%) or by another adult (8%), for example, the child's non-resident parent or another relative, who decided the child would be better off with them.

Where the children had siblings at home (in 63 of the 84 cases), just under half of the time all of the other children also moved or were removed from the family at the same time as the study child. Over half of the time, however, one or more children remained in the family home after the study child had left.

Length of the returns

The 84 returns had lasted on average seven-and-a-half months before they disrupted, with the shortest return lasting only overnight and the longest almost the full 24 months. A third of the returns had failed within three months, a further third after between four and nine months, and the final third before the end of the two-year follow-up period (see Figure 11.1).

Figure 11.1
Duration of the 84 disrupted returns (in months)

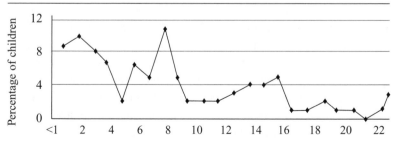

In a number of cases these returns appeared to have helped children to recognise that their parent/s were not able to care for them adequately and they had been freed up to move on to a more suitable placement, sometimes having dispelled idealised notions about their family (Fein *et al*, 1983; Thoburn, 2003).

Children's subsequent placements

After the returns ended, four-fifths (82%) of the children returned to care, whilst a fifth (18%) went to live elsewhere, such as with their other parent, a relative or friend or to live independently. Most of the children who returned to care were living in foster placements (62%), although several moved to a residential unit, either alone or occasionally with their parent/s, for further assessment.

Of the 69 children who returned to care, fewer than a fifth (17%) returned to exactly the same placement they had been in before the study return. Half went to a different placement of the same type (e.g. to a different foster carer when they had been in foster care previously) and the remaining third went to a placement of a different type (e.g. to residential care when they had been in foster care previously or vice versa).

Children's subsequent care careers

Two of the children who had absconded after the return were subsequently located and returned to care. The third absconding child was later found to be living with his other parent and remained there. Five other children, who had been living with their other parent or with friends, kin or independently, returned to care within the two-year follow-up period.

This took the total number of children in care during that time to 76 (or 42% of the total sample of children). These children experienced a great deal of instability in the time they were subsequently looked after (on average just under a year during the follow-up period), with only a quarter (28%) remaining in the same placement for the whole time and the remainder moving once (32%), twice (12%) or more (28%). These latter children experienced four or more placements during this relatively short time, with 12 per cent moving placements between five and 12 times.

Subsequent returns home from care

This instability was, in part, created by the number of children who were subsequently, unsuccessfully, returned home again. More than two-thirds of the children (68%, 47) who returned to care from the study return, were reunified again once or more during the remainder of the follow-up period, with only half (49%, 23) of those returns continuing at the end of that time (the average length of the returns was just over six months).

Of these 47 children who went on to have further returns home, 37 (79%) were returned just once, eight (17%) twice and two (4%) three times. Both of these latter returns failed a third time before the end of the follow-up period and Gemma's story below illustrates one of these stories. Indeed, the success of the returns diminished with each subsequent reunification attempt, with half (49%) being successful on the first subsequent attempt, two-fifths (40%) on the second and none on the third.

Gemma's story

At the age of 12 Gemma was described as being sullen, dishevelled and unhappy and was accommodated after her mother injured herself and was admitted to hospital under the influence of alcohol. Children's services accommodated Gemma briefly to encourage her to attend school regularly. Over the next few months, Gemma was excluded from school for aggressive behaviour and her mother was hospitalised twice after falling whilst drunk. As a result, Gemma was accommodated for the study care period but absconded home after five days (the study return) until a multi-professional case conference returned her to care. A month later Gemma again absconded home (subsequent return) but was then returned to foster care. Eight months later, when her foster carers moved, Gemma was returned home on the basis of her mother's reduced drinking and her own wishes (second subsequent return). This return only lasted two months, during which time the police were called to several domestic incidents at one of which Gemma

---

was removed under an emergency order. Two months later, she was again returned home (third subsequent return) when the local authority could not find a suitable placement for her. Gemma was later remanded to care for offending.

Most children (60%) returned to exactly the same parents on their subsequent return/s. Others, however, were returned to their other parent or a parent who had gained, changed or lost a partner. In all of the cases where the child was returned to the same carers and the return/s failed, the reasons for the breakdown of the subsequent return/s were the same as for the breakdown of the study return. In total, two-thirds (64%) of all the subsequent breakdowns were for the same reasons. Only when children were unsuccessfully returned to a different parent, or returned to different parent figures on different occasions, were different reasons for the breakdowns given. This suggests that, before subsequent returns are attempted, every effort should be made to ensure that the previous problems have been thoroughly addressed or else the outcome of the return is likely to be poor.

Subsequent care planning

No further attempts at reunification were anticipated for almost two-thirds (65%) of the children (30% of the full sample of 180 children) who remained in care at the end of the two-year follow-up period. Most (40%) had plans for long-term foster or residential care, four were permanently placed with kin, eight had been approved for adoption and one was to be helped to live independently once he reached 16.

The future was not so clear, however, for the remaining third (35%) of the children. Some had plans for imminent or eventual return to their birth families, one for shared care and a few had plans for time-limited assessment, whilst for eight children there was no clear plan.

The reunification history of all the children

These subsequent returns, however, were only part of the story when considering the full reunification history of all the children from the time of their first contact with children's services to the end of the follow-up period (or the time the case was closed or transferred).

Of the full sample of 180 children, two-fifths (38%, 69) had also been returned home unsuccessfully once or more prior to the study return. Forty-one children had returned home once previously, 18 children twice, seven children three times and three children between four and, in one case, nine times. A third of these children had been placed with their parents under care orders once or more than once when they were returned home, but the remaining two-thirds had been discharged from care on each occasion.

The average length of these previous returns was only just over a year (14.4 months) and 90 per cent had broken down within three years. Over half (55%) of these 69 returns were then followed by a further unsuccessful return in the form of the study return. The reasons for the breakdown of the study return were the same or very similar as for the previous return in most (three-quarters) of the cases. The reasons that most commonly recurred with these multiple return breakdowns were the breakdown of the parent–child relationship, the child being beyond parental control, the parent's substance misuse or mental health problems or the parents being unwilling to care. These issues therefore need to be taken seriously if children are to be prevented from oscillating in and out of care.

In total, two-thirds (64%) of the 180 children had experienced one or more failed returns over the time we followed their lives (from first contact with children's services to the end of the follow-up), including a third (35%) with two or more (see Figure 11.2). This latter third of children we termed "oscillators". One such child had endured a worrying 13 return breakdowns by the time he was 16. The reasons given for his last six return breakdowns were, in order, the child's offending behaviour, the breakdown of the parent–child relationship and then, four times, the parent's unwillingness to care. Only 65 of the 180 children (36%) had not experienced *any* disrupted returns by the end of the two-year follow-up period.

Figure 11.2
Total number of disrupted returns for full sample of 180 children

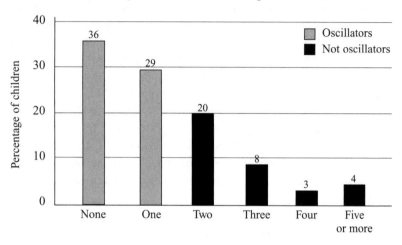

The children's perceptions of their subsequent moves and the future

Oscillation between care and home and instability in care

Concerns have been expressed about children who oscillate or move a great deal between their families and care (see, for example, Bullock *et al*, 1993; Packman and Hall, 1998; Ward and Skuse, 2001; Harwin *et al*, 2001; Sinclair *et al*, 2005), which we defined as having two or more failed returns. We were therefore interested to know how the children themselves regarded this situation. Eleven of the 19 young people we interviewed had had this experience and we had information from eight of them on this issue. All of them saw these moves as very difficult. The five children who had experienced many placements in care also reported on the negative impact of this experience.

A number of the young people expressed strong feelings about the difficulties that moving between home and care had caused them:

I felt very disturbed . . . I just didn't cope any more . . . It was just very confusing for me . . . Coming home again was very, very difficult . . . I just felt really depressed.

One young man had found it:

Very negative. I felt insulted that I'm worse than I was when I went back [into care]. I feel angry all the time and upset . . . I was confused and didn't know what was going on . . . I felt abandoned.

His reaction to care was:

Try and block everything out if you can. 'Cos don't let anything get to you. It's just going to get you down more. Fuck everyone!

Similarly, Mandy, who had returned home four times, connected this instability with her eating disorder. She said:

Going in and out of care kind of messed me up quite a bit 'cos I went through a stage of trying to commit suicide 'cos I don't want to be in care. And then right now I get really frustrated. I have holes in my wardrobe, I punch them when I get so angry . . . It wasn't very nice, 'cos it kind of interfered with my life.

Sheila felt confused and fearful as a result of moving between home and care whilst Lindy had felt 'all over the place and a bit lost'. In contrast, one young man who had had four returns home, managed by not thinking about them:

I didn't even remember I went into care and came back till today.

One young woman who had threatened suicide on a number of occasions took an outwardly robust stand:

I just dealt with it I suppose. I didn't particularly like it that much, but I just dealt with it. Got on with it basically which is all you can do. 'Cos if you kick up a fuss, it's just going to make it worse on yourself . . . It made me a stronger person. I can deal with anything now . . . Overall, it made me a stronger person.

In addition, the young people offered another more unexpected perspective on having had previous returns. They described a 'practice effect', whereby they were hardened to the difficulties they might meet and knew more about what to expect. For example, Lindy said about her second and later returns:

> *It was easier, as I knew when to keep my mouth shut and knew what it was like.*

Alice and Sheila too said that having had a previous return made the next one easier and Mandy agreed, saying that having had previous returns made this one:

> *. . . easier because I knew what was going to happen.*

Tina too felt that she had been inoculated against return breakdown:

> *I just got used to it now. So if I ever get kicked out I know I can do it. Because I've done it before basically.*

Jamie was the only young person to take a different line. He felt that having had previous returns had made it harder this time.

Some children had had many moves in care even though they had not returned home in between, whilst others had had very unstable care careers as well as oscillating between home and care. Doug thought that his many moves in care had contributed to him shouting and 'mouthing off' and letting his anger out. Two young people emphasised their fear that they would never get to return home, whilst others saw moves in care as confusing, scary and disappointing. One young woman who had been abused in care said:

> *I mean, after being with Sue and Richard [foster carers], I thought, you know, if I go into another placement, am I going to get, you know, a hand raised to me again? 'Cos it was quite scary.*

Three wishes

At the end of the interviews, we asked the young people what they would wish for if we gave them three wishes. Most of them (10 out of 15 who responded) gave wishes that concerned their family life or their past in care (see also Ward, 1995). For example, Mandy, whose mother was mentally ill, said that she wished 'to get on with my mum', whilst Julie, whose mother had almost but not completely dealt with her alcohol problem, said, 'Mum to get completely better; my sister to get a house and be happy with her life; my nephew to grow up without fears'. Children who were at home tended to wish that this would continue. For example, Tina wished that she would 'always have my mum and my family'. Carrie wanted 'Mum never to die; have a nice home and family' and Sheila wished for 'me and my family to go on a real nice holiday together', whilst Alice settled for one wish: 'Always live with my mum'.

One young person who was in substitute care wanted 'to see more of my family – father, mother and sister; to be rich; have a nice life' whilst another young man who felt marooned in care said, 'to go back to my mum; to be close to my friends; have a bit of money to spend on the family'. Sheila wanted to see more of her former foster carers.

A few young people mentioned having or staying with boyfriends or girlfriends: 'live happy ever after with my boyfriend', 'me and my girlfriend to stay together', 'get my man', whilst several mentioned their own behaviour, with one saying: 'not be so violent; to behave well at school', another, 'stay out of trouble', a third, 'be good at home' and a fourth, 'no more fighting'. Only two mentioned careers. One said she wished 'to be a nurse; get a good education', whilst the other wanted 'to do well in college at art and design'.

Jason took a somewhat different perspective in wishing 'for my past not to have happened – but then I wouldn't be the person I am'. Somewhat similarly, Jamie wished 'just to fucking have a normal life; have a family'. Two of the young people declined to respond, with one young woman who was living with her parents but was very neglected and had missed much of her schooling saying twice, 'I don't think of things like that', which seemed to convey that she did not feel sufficiently confident to imagine a brighter future.

Social workers' perceptions of the children's subsequent moves

The social workers made some interesting comments about the children who had returned home once or more after the study return.

Subsequent continuing returns

In the two cases where such subsequent returns home were continuing, social workers said that substantial work had been undertaken with the parents and children fully to address the problems, and that this was the critical factor in their success.

In one, work had been undertaken with the child and his parents on family relationships and behaviour management. In the other, a mother who wanted her daughter home had worked for two years to change her lifestyle: she went to AA and stopped drinking, ended her violent relationships, and used contact to improve her relationship with her daughter. She asked to be re-assessed and the assessment continued for six months to test her commitment and to investigate how far she had changed. In the social worker's judgement, the success of the subsequent return was entirely due to the mother accepting responsibility for herself and her daughter and engaging in work to change her life.

In contrast, a social worker regarded one child's subsequent return as of poor quality: she thought the child was worse off at home than she had been in foster care. However, the case had been closed three months after the return home because the mother would not engage in any work, even though there were continuing problems in the mother–child relationship, the child had difficulties at school and had taken two overdoses and the stepfather was alcoholic.

Subsequent disrupted returns

Five of the subsequent returns home had broken down for reasons similar to those given for the disruption of the study returns. Social workers described the ending of these returns as having a severe negative impact on three of the children. One of these children went home as a "stop gap" because no suitable placement was available for him. It ended in a major row between the young person and his parents, in which both he and his mother were physically injured. The second child, who was aged 10, returned home again shortly after the breakdown of the study return but without any resolution of the problems (father's alcoholism, violence and physical and emotional abuse of the child). The social worker's objections to the return were overruled by managers. The return broke down after the child was physically abused. The social worker believed that the third child had to check out whether another return could work out, but said 'the whole experience was traumatic' for him. She considered that each return had been even more abusive and unsettling than the previous one.

Oscillation

Some social workers commented on the severe negative impact on children of oscillating between home and care. One said that the moves had disrupted the child's ability to make relationships and another that the moves had disrupted the boy's education and increased his experience of instability.

Now that the children's subsequent returns and experiences during the follow-up period have been examined, we consider, in the final chapter, the implications for policy and practice of the study as a whole.

Summary

- By the end of the two-year follow-up period, of the 180 returns, half (47%) had ended. Parental problems were the dominant cause of returns ending. Abuse and neglect were a less frequent reason for return breakdown and there had been an increase in the number of return breakdowns attributable to the child's difficult behaviour.
- The key issues affecting parents' ability to care were the breakdown of the parent–child relationship, parental mental health problems or drug or alcohol misuse, domestic violence and relationship breakdown.
- Parents initiated the end of the returns over two-fifths of the time. The remainder of the time, the child (16%) or another adult (8%) took action or children's services (28%) or the court (5%) intervened to protect the children.
- The 84 returns had lasted on average seven-and-a-half months before they ended, with a third of the returns ending within three months, a further third after four to nine months, and the final third before the end of the two-year follow-up period.
- After the returns ended, four-fifths of the children returned to care (most to foster care) whilst a fifth (18%) went to live with their other parent, a relative or friend, or found accommodation independently.

Fewer than a fifth of the children went back to exactly the same care placement.

- Children experienced a great deal of instability whilst subsequently looked after, in part created by the number of children who were subsequently, unsuccessfully, returned home again. More than two-thirds of the children who returned to care after the study return were reunified again once or more during the follow-up period, with only half of those returns ongoing at the end of that time.
- When examining the full reunification histories of all 180 children, two-thirds (64%) had experienced one or more failed returns over the time we followed their stories, and a third (35%) two or more.

The children's and social workers' views of events during the follow-up period

- Children expressed strong feelings about the difficulties that moving between home and care had caused them. They described feeling unable to cope, feeling angry, upset and abandoned and how these moves and feelings of rejection had had a long-term effect on them. Nonetheless, they said that their previous experiences of return in some ways made the next one easier, since they knew what to expect.
- When asked for their three wishes, most children made wishes that concerned their family life or their past in care.
- Social workers described some of these returns as having a severe negative impact on the children. Some also commented on the very negative impact on children of oscillating between home and care.

12 Summary and implications for policy and practice

There has been little up-to-date information about reunification in the UK and this study aimed to fill some of these gaps in our knowledge. The research examined the characteristics, progress and outcomes of children returned home and considered the factors that contributed to good outcomes for them. The study was conducted by means of a two-year follow-up of a sample of 180 looked after children who were returned to their parent/s in a set year. The sample was drawn from six local authorities and data collection was by means of case file reviews. In addition, through interviews with a sub-sample of parents, children and social workers involved in these returns, we aimed to shed light on the needs of children and parents and on the practice issues for social workers and other professionals.

This chapter draws together the key findings from the study. Findings about planning and decision-making for reunification and return outcomes are considered as are a range of issues about reunification practice. Throughout the chapter, attention is drawn to the factors that related to returns being stable and to the implications for policy and practice. The use of the words "statistically significant" have been used sparingly in this chapter, but should generally be assumed unless stated otherwise.

The children's early experiences

The sample of children returning home from care had excluded only one group of children who were likely to be unproblematic, that is, those who returned within six weeks. It was therefore interesting to find just how troubled were the backgrounds of the parents involved. For example, over half of the mothers had been victims of abuse or neglect themselves and over a quarter had spent time in care when they were younger. Concerns about their children had typically begun early in their lives, with a quarter referred to children's services by or at birth and almost three-quarters referred by the time they started school.

The children in care

Half of the children entered care because of abuse or neglect and over a quarter because of their own behaviour. Before returning home, the majority of the children were voluntarily accommodated (59%) and by return, the remainder were subject to interim, care orders or supervision orders. As expected, children subject to court orders were significantly younger than those voluntarily accommodated.

Most children returned home from foster (71%) or kinship care (8%), but some did so from residential units or schools, whilst a small group returned to the community with their parent/s from mother and baby foster placements or residential family assessment centres. Some of the parents interviewed were dissatisfied with residential care since their children's behaviour had rarely improved and had sometimes worsened there; indeed nine per cent of the children were abused in care (by caregivers or other children), which could lead parents to remove children from placement, judging that care was unsafe.

Initial care plans

There were four distinct groups of children in terms of the relationship between their initial care plans and the time it took before they returned home. At one extreme were young people (6% of the sample) who absconded home or were removed soon after placement by dissatisfied parents before any plan had been made for them. A second group of children (41%) whose initial plan was "return home" were mostly accommodated adolescents who returned within an average of six months. In contrast, younger children whose initial plan was "time-limited assessment" (45%) were generally on care orders, considered at risk and took twice this long to get home. A final small group (8%) returned to their parents after an average of three years in care because the permanence plans made for them had not been fulfilled. The first two groups (like the others) had adverse backgrounds but they had also experienced a high number of previous returns home, yet monitoring and services for them were relatively sparse.

Planning and pressure for return

There was wide variation in terms of how much attention was paid to planning for and arranging services for reunification. In cases where the courts were involved, where young children were at risk from their parents or where an individual worker was particularly committed to the return, a number of agencies were generally involved and very intensive packages of support arranged. This was also likely to occur when children and/or parents had been in specialist assessment or treatment centres, since staff often remained involved during the return.

At the other end of the spectrum, there was sometimes little social work planning and no services arranged, especially when parents had removed children from their placements or when young people absconded home.

Very few (26%) of the returns were free from pressures of one sort or another, so the reality of practice is often planning under pressure. However, it was interesting to find that, when parents had pressed for return (and these were mostly children on care orders), there was an increased likelihood of return stability, presumably because of parental motivation to care (Cleaver, 2000; Harwin et al, 2001; Sinclair et al, 2005). So such pressure sometimes provides an opportunity for positive work with parents, as long as their main problems are being addressed.

In contrast, when children's returns were accelerated because of placement or other problems (often connected with difficult child behaviours and sometimes with absconding home) there were more return disruptions (see also Wade et al, 2011). In some cases, children were very anxious to return to their parents and this could produce increasing pressure that was hard to resist. One young person, for example, sabotaged each placement because he wanted to go home. The social worker for another child considered that she had to be allowed to try returning again to the mother, to whom she wished to return but who could not manage her. In such situations children may need their former placements in care to remain open for a period, so that they can go back to them if the return disrupts (see also Thoburn, 1994; Farmer *et al*, 2004).

Assessment and intervention

Forty-three per cent of the children returned to a parent without any in-depth assessment of their situation. Assessment was linked to service provision and to return stability. More specifically multi-agency assessments – which often led to services – were linked to the resolution of the problems that had led to care. This highlights the need for a multi-disciplinary approach given the complexity of the issues in many of the families (see also The Who Cares? Trust, 2006).

Specialist professionals saw a third of the children and almost half of the parents before the children returned home. However, in some cases referrals had been made to mental health or other professionals but did not eventuate, because the service was unavailable or parents did not keep appointments. In addition, social workers conducted direct work with a fifth of the parents and children.

Conditions for the return were set in just over a third of cases and were mostly set when children were younger, the family situation had been assessed or when the return took place during care proceedings. There were increased levels of stability when conditions had been set. Where no work was provided for any family member (23% of cases), problems tended to persist into the return. Indeed, improvement in the family situation was the main reason for return in only half of the cases.

Reservations about the returns

Professionals, including social workers, expressed concerns about as many as a third of the returns. In the interviews parents often said that they too had harboured doubts about the wisdom of return at that time and about their ability to cope, whilst children had been worried about rejection, abuse and exposure to their parents' problems when they returned.

Preparation for the returns, the involvement of caregivers and problem resolution

Specific preparations for the children's returns were made in a third of cases. However, only a third of the children (aged 4+) were recorded as having been consulted about the timing and manner of the return and some told us that they had gone home too quickly without adequate preparation. When adequate preparation for return had been made, reunification was significantly less vulnerable to disruption.

In addition, when caregivers (mostly foster carers) had developed an exceptionally supportive relationship with the parents, again there were significantly fewer return disruptions. Such exceptional support by caregivers was particularly evident in foster placements (especially those for mother and babies where subsequent return stability was high) and occasionally after in-patient psychiatric treatment. In such placements, the staff or foster carers worked with the parents and/or children to bring about change, concerned themselves with how parents and children would manage after they left, remaining available and at times involved after discharge and sometimes provided after-care services to assist the parents or children. Foster carers sometimes provided respite care after return and this was highly valued by the children and their parents (see also Aldgate and Bradley, 1999). Where such contact was sustained, the social workers often saw the foster carers as crucial to the return's success.

More involvement by foster carers and residential workers in preparing children and in providing follow-up support after reunification could prove very helpful (The Who Cares? Trust, 2006). In the US some agencies have initiated programmes with the explicit intention of developing the role of foster carers as role models and support figures for parents and it has been shown that foster carers can play positive roles as parent counsellors, parent aides and parent educators (Lee and Park, 1980; Simmons *et al*, 1981; Davies and Bland, 1981). There is an interest in similar developments in this country (see e.g. Greenfields and Statham, 2004; Cosis Brown *et al*, 2005; Department for Education and Skills, 2007). This is an area of practice that might usefully be further developed.

Many (57%) of the returns were supported with a package of services (although in a quarter no services had been provided for the parents or children whilst the child was in care). In the researchers' view, in only a quarter of the cases had all the problems for the children and their parents been addressed prior to reunion. Often, issues which had the potential to jeopardise the success of the returns remained unresolved or hidden, especially drug or alcohol problems or continuing relationships with violent partners.

The returns – change and continuity

Two-thirds of the children returned to the same parents (or parent figures) they had lived with previously, a quarter returned to a household which a parent or partner had left or joined while they were away, whilst one in 10 returned to a different parent. Other siblings had also left or joined these households so that, in total, only just over half of the children did not experience any changes in the membership of the household to which they returned.

The likelihood of return stability was significantly higher when children moved to the other parent (who generally had fewer problems than the parent/s from whom the child entered care) or when there was a change in household composition (which could mean that a new more positive male partner had joined the family or a former negative partner had left). As with Harwin et al (2001) and Wade et al (2011), there were most return disruptions when there had been no change in the com- position of the family to which the children returned. It appears therefore that what needs to be assessed is whether specific changes in the family to which children will go are likely to be better or worse for the returning child; the children who were interviewed had clear views on this which needed to be heard. The general message though is that change within families is often positive.

Given the stresses associated with making the transition from care to home, continuity in other areas of children's lives is likely to be helpful. Relatively few children (26%) changed school on return, which suggests that considerable effort is now made to maintain continuity in education, although there are occasions when a change of school can offer children a welcome fresh start (see e.g. Farmer and Moyers, 2008). Less continuity was evident in terms of day care, with more children making a change than not when they were reunified. We also found that the continuity of entering care with siblings or returning home with them was related to return stability (as it is in other kinds of placement and in previous research on reunification).

The children's experiences

Just under half of the children interviewed had not been able to maintain contact with all their friends whilst they were in placement and the same proportion lacked strong friendship networks during the returns. A third confided in no one once they had returned home, whilst a few felt like outsiders in their own families.

Returning to parental difficulties

Over three-quarters of the children were returned to parents who had previously abused or neglected them. More than four-fifths went to parents with a history of domestic violence, drug or alcohol misuse or exposure to inappropriate sexual activity[2] and more than half to a parent with mental health problems. Ten per cent of the mothers and five per cent of the fathers had learning difficulties.

Parental ambivalence (relevant to 42% of the children) and previous failed returns (which had occurred for 38%) were significantly related to return disruption (see also Farmer and Parker, 1991; National Family Preservation Network, 2003; Biehal, 2006). This highlights the need for proactive intervention to tackle children's and parents' difficulties before any renewed attempt at return.

Children's services support during the returns

Support was provided by children's services to the majority of the children's families during the return. This included financial or material support (41% of the families), assistance from family support workers (41%), respite care (24%) and attendance at play-schemes or other activity groups (12%), albeit that such help was sometimes short term.

---

[2] Inappropriate sexual activity included prostitution and the open use of pornography.

Over half of the children under school age received assistance to attend childminders or day nursery. Social workers also provided direct work to one in five of the children and parents.

Other agency services

During the return, nearly half of the parents and of the children (aged 4 +) were also provided with specialist support by other agencies, such as mental health or youth offending teams, local family centres or health professionals.

The impact of services

Families with children subject to care or supervision orders received more support than those with children who had been accommodated. In all, almost a fifth of the parents (and two-fifths of the children) did not receive any support at all during the return – either from children's services or a specialist agency – and as a result, some parents were caring for very disruptive or emotionally troubled children without any assistance. The full extent of many difficulties did not become apparent until some time into the return or after it had disrupted.

The importance of services that are tailored to specific parental/child difficulties and needs is emphasised by our findings that returns were significantly more stable when all the problems had been addressed prior to reunification, when support was adequate during the return or when specialist support was provided for the parent or for the child. These findings emphasise that appropriate specialist services and highly skilled relationship-based social work (see e.g. Forrester et al, 2008) can and do make a difference to return outcomes. This suggests the need for service arrangements and resource provision to encourage skilled practitioners to devote time to reunification.

However, there were many gaps in the services to support return, most notably insufficient help with behaviour management, especially in managing difficult adolescents, and a lack of treatment and help for parents with substance misuse problems.

A number of the social workers talked about the importance of building parents' confidence in their ability to parent their children (see also Farmer and Parker, 1991; Thoburn, 1994) and counteracting their feelings of failure. This was particularly important when parents were separated from babies or very young children, when children or young people had been looked after for long periods or when children had serious behavioural difficulties.

At the same time it is important to note that the task for social workers is very large – in their own words 'enormous', 'a huge piece of work'. A great deal of time has to be spent arranging comprehensive packages of services, liaising with other agencies, attending meetings and at times conducting direct work. Social workers sometimes visited daily or at least weekly when children were returned.

Team managers played a crucial role in supporting the social work plans and it was only with team manager support that some workers had been able to maintain the kind of intensive support packages that assisted some returns in succeeding. Where cases were closed when there were still reasons for concern about the safety and welfare of the child, there was a significantly increased risk of return breakdown. Clearly it is important that reunification is not seen as an area of low priority where resource savings can be made, especially as the alternative may be a very costly specialist placement.

It has been suggested that returns should be seen as similar to making a new placement (Farmer, 1996), and that reunification work has similarities with placement for adoption (see e.g. Maluccio *et al*, 1986; Trent, 1989) where, for example, services like an out-of-hours service from a known worker are important (see e.g. National Family Preservation Network, 2003).

It might also be useful if all decisions for return had to be either agreed by a senior manager in the authority (as is the case for children on care orders) in order to ensure consistently high standards for children or approved by a multi-disciplinary panel (The Who Cares Trust?, 2006) which would also determine the support to be provided. This could be linked to the requirement in the Care Planning Regulations (Department for Education, 2010) that children's services hold a review before voluntarily accommodated children return to their parents and that a "child in need" plan is drawn up identifying the supports and services which will be provided (Regulation 39).

Support from schools

The local authority provided educational assistance to over half of the school-age children. Some schools provided considerable support to children (and sometimes parents) and the interviews suggested that this could be important to the success of the returns.

Informal support

Good informal support for parents and/or young people was significantly related to return stability, whereas social isolation was highly associated with return disruption (Festinger, 1994). When parents or young people lack adequate support from their own networks, more professional help and support may be needed in compensation (Quinton, 2004; Farmer et al, 2004), as well as more proactive attempts to initiate and coordinate a network of informal support, possibly by means of family group conferences (Department for Education and Skills, 2007).

Monitoring and regulation during returns

Other agency professionals (e.g. health visitors or nursery staff) played a part in supervising three-fifths of the children and such monitoring was associated with return stability. Similarly, when restrictions were attached to contact, there were more stable returns (see also Sinclair, 2005). Setting conditions before or during return was also related to returns lasting but was rarely undertaken with the parents of children over the age of 11.

Of course, the situations of, say, a young abused baby and an acting out teenager are not comparable. Whilst the return of the former is clearly in the gift of the local authority and parents will often be prepared to work to meet conditions in order to achieve a return, parents are likely to be much less anxious to be reunited with their challenging or disruptive adolescent children. Nonetheless, these findings highlight that the use of conditions, set out in a written agreement, is an important part of routine reunification practice. This is in line with findings from two studies of specialist reunification projects in the US, which concluded that purposeful case planning for children's futures, working jointly with parents from the time of entry to care, combined with written contracts agreeing clear goals with parents, were vital ingredients of the projects (Stein and Gambrill, 1977, 1979; Walton et al, 1993).

The parents themselves often disliked being monitored or assessed, feeling that professionals, especially social workers, were 'digging the dirt' on them and sometimes that such control was provided without any accompanying encouragement or reassurance. Forming constructive working relationships with parents in such situations was far from easy but when it was achieved, parents were appreciative.

The children's progress at home – recurrence of parental difficulties, especially substance misuse

Once the children went home, there was considerable improvement in some areas. Domestic violence, which had featured in two-thirds of families before the children entered care, was reported in under a fifth during the two-year follow-up period, probably because mothers had separated from violent partners, whilst substance misuse, which had been an issue in three-fifths of the families, was now evident in just under a third.

However, the difficulty faced by professionals in bringing about change in parental behaviours is shown by the *recurrence* rates of these issues. Whilst domestic violence reappeared in only a fifth of cases, alcohol misuse recurred in more than half the cases and drugs misuse in two-fifths. Other issues which recurred frequently were social isolation, financial problems, poor parenting skills and poor home conditions, all of which were significantly more likely to occur where a parent was misusing drugs or alcohol. Indeed, the children of substance misusing parents were very much more likely be abused or neglected (78%) than the children of parents without these problems (29%).

Abuse and neglect

Almost half of the children (46%) were abused or neglected during the return – which was half the number who were thought to have been maltreated prior to entering care. Neglect, emotional abuse and physical abuse were particularly likely to recur, unlike sexual abuse (because perpetrators had often left the household). New occurrences of maltreatment were relatively rare, except in relation to physical abuse. Statistical analysis revealed that poor parenting skills was the greatest predictor of child maltreatment during the return (Hess *et al*, 1992; Davis *et al*, 1993; Courtney, 1995), followed by drug or alcohol misuse (Schuerman *et al*, 1994; Packman and Hall, 1998).

After concerns about maltreatment had been raised, almost a fifth of the children were immediately taken back into care. However, two-fifths of them remained at home without adequate protection, whilst 16 per cent of the children stayed at home despite ongoing maltreatment. When babies or children under five were at risk or had been physically abused, great care was usually taken to assess the parents and monitor returns, and swift action was taken if necessary to remove the children. However, practice was much less consistent as children became even a little older. The children who were least likely to be monitored adequately were those where there had been no assessment or where children were not under a child protection plan.

Most forms of difficult behaviour were more likely to recur during the return than be resolved. For example, almost half of the children exhibited behaviour problems or under-achievement or non-attendance at school or nursery during the return. Many parents struggled to cope with these behaviours and concerns about the parents' care of 69 per cent of the children were reported to children's services, by professionals, relatives and neighbours.

Nonetheless, nearly three-fifths of the children appeared to be close to a parent, although a tenth were close to only one parent and not the other, and, worryingly, a third were close to neither. A considerable number of the young people said in interview that they found things difficult at home, felt sad, confused or angry or missed their former placement.

The outcomes of the returns

By the end of the two-year follow-up period, almost half (47%) of the returns had broken down. The 84 disrupted returns had lasted an average of seven-and-a-half months. Although most of the continuing returns were rated as of good quality for the child, a quarter were borderline (where it was finely balanced as to whether or not the child would have been better off in care) and 12 per cent were of poor quality. Given this situation, there is a need for closer monitoring of return decisions and return progress within local authorities.

Legal status and adolescent returns

Children who returned home on a supervision or care order were significantly more likely to experience return stability as compared with those who were voluntarily accommodated. This is an interesting finding since these children were likely to be those thought to be most at risk of maltreatment (although presumably those at highest risk would not have been returned to their parents). However, part of the explanation for these lower levels of disruption probably relates to the younger age of these children and our finding that those on court orders received more support from children's services and other agencies, were more often set conditions to fulfil before children returned, and were subject to closer monitoring.

There was least assistance for the children and young people who were accommodated, who were generally older and in many cases adolescent. Yet they too had often experienced multiple adversities (56% had done so as compared with 67% of children on court orders) and also instability, both in care and because of repeat returns. Indeed, being over the age of 11 was strongly associated with return breakdown, as in other kinds of placement and in previous research on reunification (see e.g. Rowe et al, 1989) and also with poorer quality returns. Whilst their stays in care might have provided respite for their parents, the proportion of young people who showed improved behaviour or lessening of their difficulties was low.

The interviews revealed the particular difficulties of bringing about change in young people who had serious behaviour problems and whose parenting had often been unsatisfactory and inconsistent. Nonetheless, there were promising examples of good practice, where the placements in care had included interventions for the young people aimed at helping them to change their behaviour (and sometimes assistance for parents with behaviour management) and where the adolescents and their parents were able to access a strong network of support after return, which could include regular respite care and positive support for the young people from a mentor, teacher, a parent's new partner or a boy or girlfriend. After-care services from the placement had also helped to maintain some of these returns.

There is clearly a need for more focused work with young people with behavioural and emotional problems who enter care and with their parents and also for more consistency in arranging tailored support packages to help to make these returns work (see e.g. Biehal, 2008). Some of the techniques and "wraparound support" packages from Treatment Foster Care (see e.g. Chamberlain, 1990; Chamberlain et al, 1992; Chamberlain and Reid, 1998) might be applied to reunification, whilst the use of support care (Greenfields and Statham, 2004; Cosis Brown et al, 2005) or short breaks/respite care (Bradley and Aldgate, 1999) might play an important part in maintaining these returns, providing positive relationships for young people and avoiding oscillation in and out of care.

Parents' views of the help they need

When we asked parents what help they had needed, they prioritised: treatment for substance misuse combined with clarity about the consequences of their taking no action about their addiction; help with behaviour management and earlier recognition of their difficulties with their children; help to build up their self-confidence as parents; to be listened to and respected; monitoring of their progress that is combined with emotional warmth; direct help for children (such as mental health assistance, anger management and mentoring) respite care; and the opportunity to talk to other parents in the same situation.

Substance misuse problems

As noted earlier, there were high recurrence rates for parental alcohol and drugs misuse when children returned home and this was significantly related to children being abused and neglected during the returns (Famularo et al, 1992; Kelleher et al, 1994). This may have been because parents were not sufficiently motivated to tackle their substance misuse or because they had too little support to do so. As we have seen, only five per cent of parents were supported by drug or alcohol professionals. Often social workers believed that parents had stopped or moderated their use of alcohol or drugs before the children were returned, when they had not. There is a need for more training for social workers in the recognition of substance misuse, in assessing its nature and severity and the associated harm to children, and in making realistic assessments about prognosis that will not be overwhelmed by the "misplaced optimism" (Forrester and Harwin, 2004, p. 129) that was often evident in this and Harwin and Forrester's (2002) study. Training is also needed in undertaking appropriate interventions, case management and care planning (see e.g. Standing Conference on Drug Abuse, 1997).

Other research (Cleaver et al, 2007) has also shown low levels of referral to drug and alcohol agencies, with more referrals for drugs than for alcohol difficulties. Social workers need to be able to access specialist help for parents. Ways also need to be found to ensure that children's social workers and drug and alcohol workers work much more closely together to help parents with addictions, with the child's best interests in mind (see for example Cleaver et al, 1999; Harwin and Forrester, 2002; Velleman, 1993, 2002; Kroll and Taylor, 2003). In future, the Family Drug and Alcohol Courts which have been piloted (Department for Education and Skills, 2007) may provide an important way forward. This is especially important in view of the strong link between substance misuse and a range of other parenting problems (see e.g. Velleman and Orford, 1999; Cleaver et al, 1999; Tunnard, 2002 a and b; ACMD, 2003; Kroll and Taylor, 2003), including abuse and neglect (Kelleher et al, 1994; Chaffin et al, 1996) shown in this and other studies.

There is clearly a need to review reunification practice in cases where parents misuse alcohol or drugs, to introduce clear expectations that parents will be required to undergo treatment (see Gossop et al, 2001) before children are returned to them, and that their substance misuse is closely monitored and reviewed before and during return. The findings of the study point not just to the need for a greater use of available services and interventions but also consideration of routine drug or alcohol testing of parents with substance misuse issues prior to and during returns.

Managing unplanned returns

Some social workers made it clear that they had been unhappy about a return taking place but said that they could do nothing to stop the parents taking the children home because they were accommodated. This highlights the practice issue of how to manage and monitor cases where children's services have responsibility for children's welfare but find it difficult to exercise, either because of parental/child disengagement or resistance or because other cases are given priority (see Maluccio *et al*, 1986; Trent, 1989; Farmer and Parker, 1991; Thoburn, 1994).

Sometimes more contingency planning may be needed to consider what action the authority would take if a parent brings forward a return at a stage when it is unlikely to work. In addition, when this situation occurs, social workers should consider undertaking a full assessment of the children at home with their parents once they have returned, to see what services might be needed and to ensure the child's safety. Consideration might be given to arranging a planned change of worker, since a new practitioner might not be associated with the negative events of the past, such as the children's entry to care (Thoburn, 1994; Farmer and Owen, 1995). Engagement with the voluntary sector might provide another way forward.

Working with unco-operative parents

It was not uncommon to find that when social workers had commented that the parents were unwilling to engage in work, the parents had said that they did not get any support with the child's behaviour. In some situations, when social workers emphasised that the parents had failed to take responsibility for their children's difficulties, the parents had felt that they had simply been blamed for their children's difficult behaviour but not been helped to manage it. They had often asked for help many years earlier and felt that they had not been listened to or helped at that stage. Social workers have the difficult task of having to be clear with parents about what standards of care they need to meet for their children to return and at the same time assisting parents to see if they have the capacity to change and building up their confidence to do so. This study suggests, as have many others (see e.g. Forrester *et al*, 2008), that firmness or confrontation about parenting standards or problems needs to be combined with empathy.

Nonetheless, some of the parents were clearly extremely difficult to help and were quick to criticise others (see e.g. Thoburn *et al*, 2009). Social workers had difficulty in contacting and/or engaging the parents or children in one in five cases. Moreover, a number of the parents who had been involved in care proceedings said that they did not tell the social workers about their difficulties for fear that the children would be removed again (see also Thoburn, 1980).

Borderline cases

When children are removed from parents who have had difficulties in managing them or in keeping them safe, it is not surprising that the standards of care that these parents can achieve is not generally comparable to those we would expect if they were living with specially selected and trained foster carers. When considering the quality of the returns in the study, we had to create an intermediate classification of "borderline" cases. These were situations in which the judgement as to whether the child was better off at home (despite the serious limitations there) or would have been better off being in care was finely balanced. These borderline cases may include some of the cases which are most difficult for social workers to deal with. Nonetheless, more attention to these cases at reviews and/or before case closure might have ensured that a group of professionals carefully weighed up the obvious disadvantages of the returns against the presumed benefits to the children and that these decisions did not rest solely with individual practitioners and their managers. In addition, the children's own views of where they wanted to be need to be clearly heard, since we found that in a few borderline cases the children themselves were clear that they did not wish to remain at home.

Lack of safeguarding and the need for review

As we have seen, 16 per cent of the children remained at home despite ongoing maltreatment. It was not entirely clear why the child protection concerns in these cases were not taken more seriously. In some cases, children's services staff may have concluded that on balance the children were better off in a far from ideal home environment than they would have been in care (the issue of borderline cases) and it may also have been thought that there was insufficient evidence to initiate care proceedings, especially in the absence of a very compelling "trigger" event (Dingwall *et al*, 1983; Tanner and Turney, 2003). It can be particularly difficult to take action in situations which have been implicitly condoned for some time (Farmer and Parker, 1991). There is also the practice issue of how to maintain an accurate perspective on the extent of difficulties in the context of the habituation associated with long-term work. In other cases, children's services staff may have taken the view that there was little to offer the child and been anxious to close the case (or if the return involved a move say to another parent this might have been seen as outside their area of responsibility). However, in future the Human Rights Act (which places public authorities under a duty to protect individuals from inhuman and degrading treatment) may be used to try to sue councils which fail to remove children from an abusive home (Dyer, 2007; Munro and Ward, 2008).

Once reunification had taken place, there was a need for close review of its progress and careful re-assessment of whether parental or child difficulties emerged. In addition, as has been seen, the extent of the difficulties in some families did not become clear until some time into the return.

Oscillation

Almost two-thirds of the children who re-entered care after their returns had disrupted were reunified again, once or more during the remainder of the follow-up period. The success of the returns diminished with each subsequent attempt (and most broke down for the same reasons as before), so that previous failed return was associated with a greater likelihood of further return disruptions.

When considering the full return histories of all the 180 children in the study, we found that two-thirds of them had experienced one or more failed returns over the time we followed their histories, including more than a third with two or more. This latter third of children we termed "oscillators". One such child had endured as many as 13 return breakdowns by the time he was 16. The social workers in the interviews commented on the severe negative impact on children of oscillating between home and care, whilst the children's accounts made it clear that they felt that repeated failed returns were extremely detrimental to their welfare. These findings suggest again that before subsequent returns are attempted every effort should be made to ensure that there has been change and that the previous problems have been thoroughly addressed.

For a number of children more needed to be done to prevent a continuing pattern of oscillation between home and care. Reviews need to ensure that they pick up patterns of oscillation and consideration should then be given to intervening more decisively, for example, by earlier instigation of care proceedings in order to protect children from unplanned moves and/or by providing focused help to children and their families or specialist placements when these are needed (Farmer and Lutman, 2009).

The factors which best predicted return stability

A wide range of factors were significantly related to return stability (that is, to the return not disrupting). Using logistic regression to examine the most important of these factors when they were looked at together, the significant predictors of reunification stability that were known prior to return were that the child had not been physically abused, the child did not have a history of oscillating in and out of care (Wade et al, 2011), there was adequate preparation of the child and parent/s (see also Trent, 1989; Farmer and Parker, 1991), exceptional support was provided by the caregivers, there was pressure from parents (indicating motivation) for the child to be returned (Bullock et al, 1998; Cleaver, 2000; Harwin et al, 2001; Sinclair et al, 2005) and the local authority where the child lived.

The significant predictors of return stability after reunion were changes to the household since the child had lived there (see also Wade et *al*, 2011), the involvement of another agency or professional in the supervision of the children and their families, adequate support during return, no concerns about poor parenting (see also Hess *et al*, 1992; Davis *et al*, 1993; Courtney, 1995) and the child not showing severe attachment-type difficulties.

These factors suggest that there is a need for additional support and monitoring for children with a history of physical abuse or of oscillation in and out of care or who show serious difficulties in relationships, that changes to family membership can improve the situation for children, and that purposeful social work leading up to and during the return, including arranging or providing appropriate services and support (including specialist help for children and for parents), combined with clear monitoring of the child's progress, all contribute to returns being stable.

Different local authority policies and practice

At the start of the study our authorities had few policies on reunification, which is not unlike the situation found in our research over 20 years previously (Farmer and Parker, 1991). There appeared to be considerable variation too in the priority and resources given to reunification by the different authorities, the dispositions favoured by the courts and children's guardians (especially in relation to using care orders rather than supervision orders) and thus to practice. It was also clear that some returns were driven by attempts to make cost savings, such as through reduction in numbers of out-of-authority placements.

In this context it was interesting to find that the disruption rates for the returns in our local authorities varied widely (see also Dickens *et al*, 2007; Schofield *et al*, 2007; Sinclair *et al*, 2007). Excluding the two with small numbers of cases, breakdown rates varied from a high of 75 per cent of returns to a low of 32 per cent; similarly, the proportion of returns of good quality varied from a high of 64 per cent to a low of 10 per cent. It appears then that different practices in different authorities lead to different outcomes and this was especially evident for older children.

In view of the evidence of variable practice shown in this study – particularly in relation to older or accommodated children – there is a need for authorities to develop clearer policies and procedures to guide reunification practice for all children, whatever their legal status or age. Policies need to take account of how resources to assist in the preparation and maintenance of returns can be readily accessed. In particular, specific services to assist adolescents with behavioural and emotional difficulties are needed as well as intensive help with behaviour management for their parents. Since we found that the concerns that led to entry to care had often not been addressed, assessment and decision-making need to focus more explicitly on what needs to change before return is possible, with targets clearly set and monitored by means of using conditions, accompanied by appropriate services prior to and during the return. If parents are unable to meet the conditions set and agreed within reasonable timescales and with appropriate assistance, this may mean that they are unable to care for their children and other plans may need to be made. Standards during the return need to be agreed and regularly reviewed, with action being taken when children's quality of life at home becomes unsatisfactory or when they oscillate between home and care.

Conclusion

Reunification in the UK has for long suffered from neglect in policy, research and practice. Indeed, it could be argued that there is so little attention to it that much of the time policy makers and practitioners do not conceptualise this as a specific area of their work. This needs to change. The findings of this study suggest that appropriate assessment, preparation and service are linked to returns succeeding. Lack of appropriate intervention, on the other hand, has far-reaching consequences for children's future well-being and stability. A "refocus" of attention onto reunification is therefore needed if children's outcomes are to be improved.

References

ACMD (2003) *Hidden Harm: Responding to the needs of children of problem drug users*, Report of an inquiry by the Advisory Council on the Misuse of Drugs, London: Home Office

Aldgate J. (1977) 'The Identification of Factors Influencing Children's Length of Stay in Care', PhD thesis, Edinburgh: University of Edinburgh

Aldgate J. and Bradley H. (1999) *Supporting Families through Short-term Fostering*, London: The Stationery Office

Barn R. (1993) *Black Children in the Public Care System*, London: BAAF/Batsford

Barth R. P. and Berry M. (1987) 'Outcomes of child welfare services since permanence planning', *Social Service Review*, 61, pp 71–90

Berridge D. (1997) *Foster Care: A research review*, London: The Stationery Office

Biehal N. (2006) *Reuniting looked after children with their families: A review of the research*, London: National Children's Bureau

Biehal N. (2008) 'Preventive services for adolescents: exploring the process of change', *British Journal of Social Work*, 38:3, pp 441–461

Block N. M. and Libowitz A. S. (1983) *Recidivism in Foster Care*, New York: Child Welfare League of America

Bradley M. and Aldgate J. (1999) 'Short-term family based care for children in need', in Hill M. (ed) *Signposts in Fostering: policy, practice and research issues*, London: British Agencies for Adoption and Fostering

Brandon M., Thoburn J., Rose S. and Belderson P. (2005) *Living with Significant Harm: A follow-up study*, Final Report for NSPCC, London: NSPCC

Bullock R., Little M. and Millham S. (1993) *Going Home: The return of children separated from their families*, Aldershot: Dartmouth

Bullock R., Gooch D. and Little M. (1998) *Children Going Home: The reunification of families*, Aldershot: Ashgate

Chaffin M., Kelleher K. and Hollenberg H. (1996) 'Onset of physical abuse and neglect: psychiatric, substance abuse and social risk factors from prospective community data', *Child Abuse and Neglect*, 20:3, pp 191–203

Chamberlain P. (1990) 'Comparative evaluation of a specialized foster care for seriously delinquent youths: A first step', *Community Alternatives*, 2:2, pp 21–36

Chamberlain P., Moreland S. and Reid K. (1992) 'Enhanced services and stipends for foster parents: Effects on retention rates and outcomes for children', *Child Welfare*, 71:5, pp 387–401

Chamberlain P. and Reid J. B. (1998) 'Comparison of two community alternatives to incarceration for chronic juvenile offenders', *Journal of Consulting and Clinical Psychology*, 66, pp 624–633

Child Welfare Information Gateway (2006) *Family Reunification: What the evidence shows*, Washington DC, US: Department of Health and Human Services

Cleaver H. (2000) *Fostering Family Contact*, London: The Stationery Office

Cleaver H., Unell I. and Aldgate J. (1999) *Children's Needs – Parenting Capacity*, London: The Stationery Office

Cleaver H., Nicholson D., Tarr S. and Cleaver D. (2007) *Child Protection, Domestic Violence and Parental Substance Misuse: Family experiences and effective practice*, London: Jessica Kingsley Publishers

Cosis Brown H., Fry E. and Howard J. (2005) *Support Care: How family placements can keep children and families together*, Lyme Regis: Russell House Publishing

Courtney M. E. (1995) 'Re-entry to foster care of children returned to their families', *Social Service Review*, pp 226–241

Davidson-Arad B. (2010) 'Four perspectives on the quality of life of children at risk kept at home and removed from home in Israel', *British Journal of Social Work*, 40:6, pp 1719–1735

Davies L. J. and Bland D. 'The use of foster parents as role models for parents', in Sinanoglu P. A. and Maluccio A. N. (1981) *Parents of Children in Placement: Perspectives and programs*, New York: Child Welfare League of America

Davis I. P., English D. J. and Landsverk J. A. (1993) *Going Home – and Returning to Care: A study of foster care reunification*, San Diego, CA: San Diego State University, College of Health and Human Services, School of Social Work and the Child and Family Research Group.

Department for Education (2010) *The Children Act 1989 Guidance and Regulations, Volume 2 Care Planning, Placement and Case Review*, London: Department of Education

Department for Education and Skills (June 2007) *Care Matters: Time for change*, Cm. 7137, London: Secretary of State for Education and Skills

Department of Health (1991) *Patterns and Outcomes in Child Placements*, London: HMSO

Dickens J., Howell D., Thoburn J. and Schofield G. (2007) 'Children starting to be looked after by local authorities in England: an analysis of inter-authority variation and case-centred decision making', *British Journal of Social Work*, 37:4, pp 597–617

Dingwall R., Eekelaar J. and Murray T. (1983) *The Protection of Children: State intervention and family life*, Oxford: Blackwell

Dyer C. (2007) '£100,000 for abused siblings council failed to take into care', *Guardian*, 17 September 2007

Famularo R., Kincherff R. and Fenton T. (1992) 'Parental substance abuse and the nature of child maltreatment', *Child Abuse and Neglect*, 61:4, pp 475–483

Fanshel D. and Shinn E. (1978) *Children in Foster Care*, New York: Columbia University Press

Farmer E. (1992) 'Restoring children on court orders to their families: lessons for practice', *Adoption and Fostering*, 16:1, pp 7–15

Farmer E. (1996) 'Family reunification with high risk children: lessons from research', *Children and Youth Services Review*, 18:4/5, pp 403–424

Farmer E. (2009) 'Reunification with birth families', in Schofield G. and Simmonds J. (eds) *The Child Placement Handbook: Research, policy and practice*, London: BAAF

Farmer E. and Parker R. (1991) *Trials and Tribulations: Returning children from local authority care to their families*, London: HMSO

Farmer E. and Owen M. (1995) *Child Protection Practice: Private risks and public remedies, a study of decision-making, intervention and outcome in child protection work*, London: HMSO

Farmer E. and Pollock S. (1998) *Sexually Abused and Abusing Children in Substitute Care*, Chichester: Wiley.

Farmer E. and Moyers S. (2008) *Kinship Care: Fostering effective family and friends placements*, London: Jessica Kingsley Publishers

Farmer E. and Lutman E. (2009) *Case Management and Outcomes for Neglected Children Returned to Their Parents: A five year follow-up study*, Report to the Department for Education, Bristol: University of Bristol

Farmer E. and Dance C. with Beecham J., Bonin E. and Ouwejan D. (2010) *An Investigation of Family Finding and Matching in Adoption*, Report to the Department for Children, Schools and Families, School for Policy Studies, Bristol: University of Bristol

Farmer E., Moyers S. and Lipscombe J. (2004) *Fostering Adolescents*, London: Jessica Kingsley Publishers

Fein E., Maluccio A., Hamilton V. and Ward D. (1983) 'After foster care: outcomes of permanence planning for children', *Child Welfare*, LXII, pp 485–558

Fernandez E. and Delfabbro P. (2010) 'Reunification in Australia: insights from South Australia and New South Wales', in Fernandez E. and Barth R. P. (eds) *How does Foster Care Work? International evidence on outcomes*, London: Jessica Kingsley Publishers

Festinger T. (1994) *Returning to Care: Discharge and re-entry into foster care*, Washington DC: Child Welfare League of America

Fisher M., Marsh P. and Phillips D. (1986) *In and Out of Care*, London: Batsford/British Agencies for Adoption and Fostering

Forrester D. and Harwin J. (2004) 'Social work and parental substance misuse', in Phllips R. (ed) *Children Exposed to Parental Substance Misuse: Implications for family placement*, London: BAAF

Forrester D. and Harwin J. (2008) 'Parental substance misuse and child welfare. Outcomes for children two years after referral', *British Journal of Social Work*, 38:8, pp 1518–1535

Forrester D., Kershaw S., Moss H. and Hughes L. (2008) 'Communication skills in child protection: how do social workers talk to parents?', *Child and Family Social Work*, 13, pp 41–51

Fraser M. W., Walton E., Lewis R. E., Pecora P. J. and Walton W. K. (1996) 'An experiment in family reunification: correlates of outcomes at one-year follow-up', *Children and Youth Services Review*, 18:4/5, pp 335–361

Fratter J., Rowe J., Sapsford D. and Thoburn J. (1991) *Permanent Family Placement: A decade of experience*, London: British Agencies for Adoption and Fostering

Gibbons J., Conroy S. and Bell C. (1995) *Operating the Child Protection System. A study of child protection practices in English local authorities*, London: HMSO

Goerge R. (1990) 'The reunification process in substitute care', *Social Services Review*, LXIV, pp 422–457

Gossop M., Marsden J. and Stewart D. (2001) *NTORS After Five Years. The National Treatment Outcome Study. Changes in substance use, health and criminal behaviour during the five years after intake*, London: National Addiction Centre

Greenfields M. and Statham J. (2004) *Support Foster Care: Developing a short-break service for children in need*, Understanding Children's Social Care 8, London: Thomas Coram Unit

Haringey Local Children Safeguarding Board (2008) *Serious Case Review: Child 'A'*, Executive Summary, London: London Borough of Haringey

Haringey Local Children Safeguarding Board (2009) *Serious Case Review: Baby Peter*, Executive Summary, London: London Borough of Haringey

Harris P. (2008) 'Engaging substance misusers through coercion', *The Carrot or the Stick? Towards effective practice with involuntary clients in safeguarding children work*, M C Calder. Dorset: Russell House Publishing, pp 277–296

Harwin J. (2009) *The Family Drug and Alcohol Court (FDAC) Evaluation Project*, Interim Report, Report to the Nuffield Foundation and Home Office, London: Brunel University

Harwin J. Owen M., Locke R. and Forrester D. (2001) *Making Care Orders Work. A study of care plans and their implementation*, London: The Stationery Office

Harwin J. and Forrester D. (2002) *Parental Substance Misuse and Child Welfare: A study of social work with families in which parents misuse drugs and alcohol*, London: First stage report for the Nuffield Foundation (unpublished)

Hess P. M., Folaron G. and Jefferson A. B. (1992) 'Effectiveness of family reunification services: an innovative evaluative model', *Social Work*, 37:4, pp 304–311

Home Office (2008) *Drugs: Protecting families and communities – the 2008 drug strategy (first edition)*, London: Home Office. http://drugs.homeoffice.gov.uk/publications

Kelleher K., Chaffin M., Hollenberg J. and Fischer E. (1994) 'Alcohol and drug disorders among physically abusive and neglectful parents in a community based sample', *American Journal of Public Health*, 84:10, pp 1586–1590

Kendall S., Rodger J. and Palmer H. (2010) *The use of whole family assessment to identify the needs of families with multiple problems*, London: DfE [online]. Available: http://www.education.gov.uk/research/data/uploadfiles/DFE-RR045 .pdf October, 2010], Website: Department for Education (DfE)

Kroll B. and Taylor A. (2003) *Parental Substance Misuse and Child Welfare*, London: Jessica Kingsley Publishers

Lahti J. (1982). 'A follow-up study of foster children in permanent placements', *Social Service Review*, 56, pp 556–71

Lee J. A. B. and Park D. N. (1980) *Walk a Mile in My Shoes – A Manual on Biological Parents for Foster Parents*, Harford W., Connecticut: Center for the Study of Child Welfare, University of Connecticut

Lynskey M. T., Fergusson D. M. and Horwood J. L. (1994) 'The effects of parental alcohol problems on the rates of adolescent psychiatric disorders', *Addiction*, 89, pp 1277–1286

Maluccio A. N., Fein E. and Olmstead K. A. (1986) *Permanence Planning for Children: Concepts and methods*, New York: Tavistock

Maluccio A. N., Fein E. and Davis I. P. (1994) 'Family reunification: research findings, issues and direction', *Child Welfare*, Vol. LXXIII, No. 5, pp 489–504

Maluccio A. N. and Ainsworth F. (2003) 'Drug use by parents: a challenge for family reunification practice', *Children and Youth Services Review*, 25:7, pp 511–533

McMurtry S. and Lie G. Y. (1992) 'Differential exit rates of minority children in foster care', *Social Work Research and Abstracts*, 28:1, pp 42–48

McSherry D., Weatherall K., Larkin E., Malet M. F. and Kelly G. (2010) 'Who goes where? Young children's pathways through care in Northern Ireland', *Adoption and Fostering*, 34, pp 23–37

Millham S., Bullock R., Hosie K. and Little M. (1986) *Lost in Care: The problems of maintaining links between children in care and their families*, Aldershot: Gower

Moyers S., Farmer E. and Lipscombe J. (2006) 'Contact with family members and its impact on adolescents and their foster placements', *British Journal of Social Work*, 36:4, pp 541–559

Munro E. R. and Ward H. (2008) 'Balancing parents' and very young children's rights in care proceedings: decision-making in the context of the Human Rights Act 1998', *Child and Family Social Work*, 13:2, pp 227–234

National Black Child Development Institute (1993) *Parental Drug Abuse and African American Children in Foster Care: Issues and Findings*, Washington DC: NBCDI

National Family Preservation Network (2003) *Intensive Family Reunification Services Protocol*, Idaho: Buhl

Packman J. and Hall C. (1998) *From Care to Accommodation: Support, protection and control in child care services*, London: The Stationery Office

Pinkerton J. (1994) *In Care at Home*, Aldershot: Avebury

Quinton D. (2004) *Supporting Parents: Messages from research*, London: Jessica Kingsley Publishers

Quinton D., Rushton A., Dance C. and Mayes D. (1997) 'Contact between children placed away from home and their birth parents: research issues and evidence', *Clinical Child Psychology and Psychiatry*, 2:3, pp 393–413

Quinton D., Rushton A., Dance C. and Mayes D. (1998) *Joining New Families: A study of adoption and fostering in middle childhood*, Chichester: Wiley

Rowe J., Hundleby M. and Garnett L. (1989) *Child Care Now. A survey of placement patterns*, London: British Agencies for Adoption and Fostering

Rzepnicki T. L., Schuerman J. R. and Johnson P. (1997) 'Facing uncertainty: reuniting high-risk families', in (ed) Berrick J. D., Barth R. P. and Gilbert N., *Child Welfare Research Review*, Vol 2, New York: Columbia University Press

Scannapieco M. and Jackson S. (1996) 'Kinship care: the African American response to family preservation', *Social Work*, 41:2, pp 190–196

Schofield G., Thoburn J., Howell D. and Dickens J. (2007), 'The search for stability and permanence: modelling the pathways of long-stay looked after children', *British Journal of Social Work*, 37, pp 619–642

Schuerman J. R., Rzepnicki T. L. and Johnson P. R. (1994) *Outcomes in Evaluation of the 'Family First' Reunification Program of the Department of Children and Family Services*, Final Report, Chicago: Chapin Hall Centre for Children at the University of Chicago

Simmons G., Gumpert J. and Rothman B. (1981) 'Natural parents as partners in child care placement', in Sinanoglu P. A. and Maluccio A. N. *Parents of Children in Placement: Perspectives and programs*, New York: Child Welfare League of America

Sinclair I. (2005) *Fostering Now: Messages from research*, London: Jessica Kingsley Publishers

Sinclair I. and Gibbs I. (1998) *Children's Homes: A study in diversity*, Chichester: Wiley

Sinclair I., Baker C., Wilson K. and Gibbs I. (2005) *Foster Children: Where they go and how they get on*, London: Jessica Kingsley Publishers

Sinclair I., Baker C., Lee J. and Gibbs I. (2007) *The Pursuit of Permanence: A study of the English care system*, London: Jessica Kingsley Publishers

Sinclair R., Garnett L. and Berridge D. (1995) *Social Work and Assessment with Adolescents*, London: National Children's Bureau

Skuse T. and Ward H. (2003) *Listening to Children's Views of Care and Accommodation*, Report to the Department of Health, Centre for Child and Family Research, Loughborough: University of Loughborough

Smith G. (1995) *The Protectors' Handbook: Reducing the risk of child sexual abuse and helping children recover*, London: The Women's Press

Standing Conference on Drug and Alcohol Abuse (SCODA) (1997) *Drug Using Parents: Policy guidelines for inter-agency working*, London: Local Government Association Publications

Stein, M (2009) *Quality Matters in Children's Services: Messages from research*, London: Jessica Kingsley Publishers

Stein T. J. and Gambrill E. D. (1977) 'Facilitating decision-making in foster care: the Alameda Project', *Social Service Review*, September 1977, pp 502–513

Stein T. J. and Gambrill E. D. (1979) 'The Alameda Project: a two year report and one year follow-up', *Child Abuse and Neglect*, 3, pp 521–528

Sturgess W., Dunn J. and Davies L. (2001) 'Young children's perceptions of their relationships with family members: links with family setting, friendships, and adjustment', *International Journal of Behavioral Development*, November 25, pp 521–529

Tanner K. and Turney D. (2003) 'What do we know about child neglect? A critical review of the literature and its application to social work practice', *Child and Family Social Work*, 8, pp 25–34

Taussig H. N., Clyman R. B. and Landsverk J. (2001) 'Children who return home from foster care: a 6-year prospective study of behavioral health outcomes in adolescence', *Pediatrics*, 108:1, E10

Thoburn J. (1980) *Captive Clients: Social work with families of children home on trial*, London: Routledge and Kegan Paul

Thoburn J. (1994) *Child Placement: Principles and practice*, Suffolk: Arena

Thoburn J. (2003) 'The risks and rewards in adoption for children in the public care', *Family Law Quarterly*, 15:4, pp 391–402

Thoburn J. and members of Making Research Count Consortium (2009) *Effective Interventions for Complex Families where there are Concerns about, or Evidence of, a Child Suffering Significant Harm*, C4EO Safeguarding Briefing 1. www.c4eo.org.uk

Trent J. (1989) *Homeward Bound: The rehabilitation of children to their birth parents*, Ilford: Barnardo's

Tunnard J. (2002a) *Parental Drug Misuse: A review of impact and intervention studies*, Dartington: Research in Practice

Tunnard J. (2002b) *Parental Problem Drinking and its Impact on Children*, Dartington: Research in Practice

Turner J. (1984) 'Predictors of recidivism in foster care: exploratory models', *Social Work Research and Abstracts*, 20:2, pp 15–20

Velleman R. (1993) *Alcohol and the Family*, London: Institute of Alcohol Studies

Velleman R. (2002) *The Children of Problem Drinking Parents: An executive summary*, Executive Summary Series, London: Centre for Research on Drug and Health Behaviour, Executive Summary 70, pp 1–5

Velleman R. and Orford J. (1999) *Risk and Resilience: Adults who were the children of problem drinkers*, Amsterdam: OPA

Vernon J. and Fruin D. (1986) *In Care: A study of social work decision making*, London: National Children's Bureau

Wade J., Biehal N., Farrelly N. and Sinclair I. (2011) *Caring for Abused and Neglected Children: Making the right decisions for reunification or long-term care*, London: Jessica Kingsley Publishers

Walton E., Fraser M. W., Lewis R. E. and Pecora P. J. (1993) 'In-home family-focused reunification: an experimental study', *Child Welfare*, 72:5, pp 473–87

Ward H. (ed) (1995) *Looking After Children: Research into practice*, The Second Report to the Department of Health on Assessing Outcomes in Child Care, London: HMSO

Ward H. (2009) 'Patterns of instability: moves within the English care system: their reasons, contexts and consequences', *Child and Youth Services Review*, 31, pp 1113–18

Ward H. and Skuse T. (2001) 'Performance targets and stability of placements for children long looked after away from home', *Children and Society*, Vol. 15, pp 333–346

Ward H., Holmes L. and Soper J. (2008) *Costs and Consequences of Placing Children in Care*, London: Jessica Kingsley Publishers

Ward H., Brown R., Westlake D. and Munro E. R. (2010) *Very Young Children at Risk of Significant Harm: A prospective, longitudinal study*, Centre for Child and Family Research, Loughborough: University of Loughborough

The Who Cares? Trust (2006) *The Journey Home: How children's services can support the reunification of children with their families*, London: The Who Cares? Trust

Wulczyn F. (1991) 'Caseload dynamics and foster care re-entry', *Social Service Review*, 65, pp 133–156

Wulczyn F. (2004) 'Family reunification', *Children, Families, and Foster Care*, 14:1, pp 95–113

Wulczyn F. H. and Goerge R. M. (1992) 'Foster care in New York and Illinois: the challenge of rapid change', *Social Service Review*, 66, pp 278–294

Wulczyn F., Hislop K. and Goerge R. (2000), 'An update from the Multistate Foster Care Data Archive: foster care dynamics 1983–1998', Chicago, IL: Chapin Hall Center for Children, University of Chicago. Retrieved June 20, 2007, from http://www.chapinhall.org/content_director.aspx?arid=1322&afid=75&dt=1

Index